Passages to Epiphany

Journeys of Discovery and Delight

Susan Crossman

Manor House

Passages to Epiphany

Library and Archives Canada Cataloguing in Publication

Crossman, Susan
          Passages to epiphany : journeys of discovery and delight
/ Susan Crossman.

ISBN 978-1-897453-22-3

          1. Self-realization. 2. Epiphanies. 3. Crossman, Susan--
Anecdotes. I. Title.

 BF637.S4C79 2012   158.1   C2012-907725-9

Published November 15, 2012: Manor House Publishing Inc., 452 Cottingham Crescent, Ancaster, ON, CANADA, L9G 3V6   905-648-2193   wwww.manor-house.biz

All rights reserved

Cover Design: Donovan Davie based on original art by Maksim Shmeljov/Shutterstock

We acknowledge the financial support of the Government of Canada through the Canada Book Fund (CBF) for our publishing activities.

For the three people I admire most in the world:

Heather Christie
Michael Quigley
and
Michelle Quigley

Author's Note:

I put together this collection of stories as an exploration of spirit and discovery and it's been an interesting journey to say the least. I've included short fictional stories about people I've never met with personal accounts of the path I myself have tread over the past few years. I've thrown in a couple of travel pieces that relate to some of the real-world journeys of the spirit I've taken and, voilà, *Passages to Epiphany*. I've noted at the beginning of each story whether it's a real-life or fictional piece. I wish you all the best for interesting journeys of your own. May you live, learn and grow in joy and comfort.

- Susan Crossman

Foreword

By Jennifer Hough

It takes courage to go to that most vulnerable place inside of us, and express the ideas and events in our lives on paper in a way that moves the reader to new heights of awareness. There is a purity of heart and intention that seems to create an intangible almost multi-dimensional communication. It is that depth of communication that transcends words on paper and leaves our lives permanently altered. Susan Crossman has that innate ability to communicate far beyond words on paper. Having read Susan's *Shades of Teale* and this work of art, methinks there may be a pure hearted courageous genius author in our midst.

I've known Susan Crossman personally for the past several years and witnessed her expansive life blossom before my eyes, not realizing what a virtuoso of the written word was in my presence. Then I read about the profound journey of a woman named Teale (from *Shades of Teale*, Susan's last book). Having experienced Susan's writing, it is a distinct pleasure and privilege to be asked to write the Foreword to this book.

In *Awakenings*, I felt my hand being held through some very personal experiences. It's always fascinating to observe myself laughing and crying within one paragraph. Susan describes her personal experiences with love, children and regular "life"– the stuff we all go through. On reading Susan's full circle moments, there were several times I brought my own understanding of relationships to an upgraded conclusion. I had two distinct types of experiences when those full circles moments occurred. One, experience (and I'm sure you can relate) concluded in a knowing smile, as if to say "oh ya, I knew this, thanks for reminding me more deeply." The other experience was more like a full body sensation of relief, as if I had been asking for someone to show me a deeper truth, and there it was expressed in plain view as if it had been there the whole time waiting to be realized.

I deeply enjoyed the short fictional stories at the end of the book, where the characters seemed so real. Stories are like music. They have the capacity to take us on a journey. My favourite stories are those that take us on a journey, not realizing the story is actually about us, and we start to think that the author magically must have read our metaphysical biography, a record of which must be in a secret etheric library somewhere! That thought occurred to me several times as I read. It's an awakening moment to even know that awakenings are possible through simply by reading the written word.

There are two different kinds of awakenings as far as I can see: an epiphany of mental awareness about the world and an awakening of the deeper truth within us. Epiphanies are like homeopathic remedies. A vial of little sugar pellets infused with the perfect frequency to break apart emotional or physical density in one fell swoop. Very much like a laser beam to a kidney stone, or a tuning fork to a glass that resonates perfectly with the note being communicated so much so that it can no longer maintain its prior form and in an instant, it shatters. The beauty of epiphanies is that the old perspective can never hold the same power, because our minds have been shown a more resonant way of seeing our lives. Epiphanies are a glorious form of delicious relief from the chains of the past.

Having spent the last several decades diving into the world of *Awakening*, I've attempted many times to define the meaning of that word as well. Then I realized that you cannot define awakening without defining the experience. It's become clear that those moments of awakening are moments where we are freed from the dense jail of the past, old paradigms and belief systems that no longer serve us. Some people call them 'aha's', but I think 'aha's' are more like epiphanies. In an awakening moment, there is an instant we experience a deeply conscious Truth about the same old story. By allowing that greater truth to permeate the core of our cells, it displaces our old tired perspective and in an instant, we are freed from our ancestry, identities and unseen veils. I felt that newly found freedom was handed to me over and over again as I turned the pages of Susan's book. I'm in awe of her innate ability to bring readers to the brink of pure potential, and then walk us right through the door as if it was the most natural thing on earth. Hooray for 'aha's' and awakening moments.

I don't know if Susan realizes this, but I posted an incognito picture of her in the banner at the top of my Facebook fan page last year. It's a picture of Susan silhouetted against a glorious sunset on a California beach with her arms open wide, as if to say "YES YES YES" to life. Having had the privilege of getting to know Susan personally, I was very aware of her story when I took this picture. While editing the picture, a flood of small vignettes passed before my eyes about what she had transmuted, her family history, romantic entanglements, and the many ways she'd expressed that she had (along with so many women) carried others. But this woman on the beach was totally free. A powerful metaphor for me, but more importantly, I had this feeling that by posting that picture for the world to see, the metaphor would have the same freeing affect on others as it did on me. Thank you Susan for saying "YES YES YES" by sharing your life and timeless stories in a way that will truly last forever.

- **Jennifer Hough**, author, *Awakenings*

Aspects of Awakening – An Introduction

A big fat gray squirrel balanced himself on the snow bank just outside my kitchen window and twitched his bushy tail. My little friend was clutching a nut in his paws with great authority and he was gnawing at it with energy and skill. Little flecks of brown scattered onto the snow at his feet as he pried the meat from its shell.

The sun shone high in a brilliant blue sky that day, and its rays glanced off the snow and splintered into a billion glittering crystals. I stared intently at the scene beyond the borders of my house and I drank in the beauty, the peace and the radiance of what had been put before me. I felt full of gratitude for that precious morsel of visual delight and I promised myself I would return to the memory of that sweet little squirrel later in the day, as often as possible in fact, as a reminder that good things can still exist in the middle of trauma.

This was a moment of awakening for me, a moment where it felt like a veil had been lifted from my understanding to usher me into a larger awareness of the world around me. I could see there was much more available to me in life than the burdens that were engulfing me at the time and although I was choking back tears, my load was significantly lightened by the small gift of peace the squirrel had given me.

I held my breath and marvelled at the many different colours in that little squirrel's fur, at his perfectly matched eyes and the audacious fluffiness of his beautiful fat tail. I could see the delicate detail of his claws as he wrapped them firmly around his treasure. I felt connected to his world in a novel and touching way. I had never looked at an animal so intently before. The sight of him took my breath away.

After a few minutes, the squirrel bounded gracefully away, perhaps to find another nut, or play on the fence that ran around the perimeter of our backyard. I returned to rinsing the hypodermic syringe that I had just used to inject my dying husband's arm with morphine, and I took three deep breaths. There was still much to endure that endless day, and now I had been given a gift that would help ferry me through it.

I've had many moments I would call "awakenings" prior to and since that painful passage nearly five years ago. My beloved husband did ultimately pass away, as we all must in turn, and my children and I journeyed on into new lives filled with both challenges and opportunities. I haven't always seen the bright side of the road, let alone walked on it. And I haven't always felt blessed by a soaring spirit. But I have been consistently aware of those moments when a little part of me said "Aha!" as some new knowledge, insight or understanding floated into my orbit.

I'm not sure what the spiritual gurus of the world would call that type of experience but I believe it does have something to do with spirit — and that it also relates to something I personally recognize as Divine. These moments of awakening have sometimes been set in motion by visitors that have sauntered at random into my conscious awareness: a beautiful blossom standing proudly in a patch of weeds; sunshine peeking out through a sky full of ominous clouds; the glory of a starry night; an arresting strain of music.

But that's only one dimension of what I consider an awakening.

There is so much more.

A few weeks ago, I was walking my dog along one of the streets in my neighbourhood, and I was enjoying the chance for a little exercise. A man in a car stopped and asked for directions to a street he asserted was in my area. I frowned and apologized – I'd never heard of that street before.

The next day, while in my car, I drove past the very street he'd been seeking and was astonished to find that it was just a few blocks from my house. I felt a little sheepish to think that I hadn't even seen it before. But it had been there all along and I had not awakened to its existence until a stranger had expanded my awareness of its existence.

A lot of things in life are like that.

Many of us know people who were friends with someone for months or even years before they suddenly one day awoke to the fact that they were strongly attracted, or even in love with, that person. I dated my second husband for ages before realizing I had feelings for him. The more I got to know him, the more I appreciated him. Eventually I awoke into feelings of love for him. He had been there all along, and he hadn't changed, that I could tell. But my feelings for and awareness of him evolved to a point where I was able to "see" him as a partner.

We can awaken to intellectual understandings as well. Some of my favourite moments in parenting have occurred when my children finally stumbled onto the mysteries of reading. It was thrilling to watch their eyes light up as they made sense of language and opened the door to the huge new worlds of opportunity that it ultimately permits. And in the same vein, I've always loved watching those first few glides on a swing that resulted from the careful coordination of arms, legs and body weight. And the first few wobbly pushes of the pedals that allow a child to rocket forward on a two-wheeler for the first time? Magical!

As I've watched my children awaken into mastery of all of these accomplishments, and so many more, I've been struck by the excitement that goes along with developing a new understanding of self. It has been amazing to watch them "wake up" to who they are and what they can accomplish.

But awakening doesn't stop there. I believe that we can awaken into a deeper spiritual awareness of our reality as well, and we come to that point in our evolution when we realize we are not alone in this world. Not everyone embraces the idea of a God/Goddess/Source/Universe/or Creator.

And what's true for me need never be true for anyone else. But I think that a person engaged in a quest for spiritual understanding is focused on lifting the veils that cloak the answer to the question of who they really are and why they're really here. At some point in our lives many of us wonder about the concept of a Higher Power.

So far in my life, I've had a front row seat at three births and three deaths, and these experiences have left me in awe of the majesty of life and death, and the symmetry of beginnings that are also endings and endings that are also beginnings.

In my understanding of the world, there is a rolling force of creation out there and in here, inside me, and in throwing myself into the arms of the Universe I am able to fully experience something I might call the love of God.

Awakening to the nature of my own soul is an ongoing process and I'm grateful for all the mentors that have filled, and are filling, my world with possibilities.

The mystery of it all fascinates me. As any awakening does, spiritual or otherwise.

In so many areas of life we are given the opportunity to "wake up" to an appreciation of something that already exists, and it gives us the opportunity to know or feel something that we didn't know or feel before. We "wake up" to possibility and appreciation in almost any realm:

We can awaken into new tastes in music, food and clothes, or to an appreciation of new aspects of beauty, compassion, strength or wisdom.

We can awaken to an appreciation of simplicity or an understanding of complexity.

We can awaken to how much we are all the same or how much we are all so different. Or how amazing it is that so many different linguistic and cultural groups can co-exist on a planet that from deep space looks small, unremarkable and uniform.

We can awaken to a new respect for rules or a total disregard for them.

We can awaken through careful reflection about something that happened days, weeks or years previously, or be jolted awake by a sudden flash of inspiration.

We can awaken into our purpose in this life (if indeed we feel we need one) or we can awaken into the limitless field of possibility that lies just outside the boundaries of our awareness.

But the bottom line is this: if we are learning and growing, we are awakening to something, somewhere. We are changing the boundaries that have limited and contained our knowledge, understanding, awareness and beliefs, and we are pushing the envelope of our sense of self outward and skyward.

We are opening ourselves to new opportunities, concepts and ways of being, and adding ever more variety to our behavioral playlist; we have the opportunity to provide ourselves with more options we can use to design our lives. We are creating flexibility.

And, in the straightforward mathematics of the evolution of the species, the most flexible organism wins.

Which doesn't mean that it's *preferable* to awaken. There is no such thing as the "enlightenment Olympics" as my friend and mentor Jennifer Hough likes to say. Some of us are open to change and some of us are not. Not everybody cares about options, flexibility, boundaries or awakening.

We live in a complex world that is characterized by responsibility and commitment. Many of us race through our days in a stress-induced mottle of regrets about the past and worries about the future. We're already doing the best we can to lead a good life. How could "awakening" ever put food on the table?

But resisting change doesn't mean it goes away.

I think the most powerful awakenings are always unexpected.

When I was 21 I suffered a spontaneous detachment of my left retina and I came within hours of going blind in that eye. An eight-hour operation miraculously saved my sight and I spent eight weeks recuperating. The experience invited me to wake up to the priceless value of vision — which I had up until that moment taken somewhat for granted — and there hasn't been a day since then that I haven't felt enormously grateful.

I didn't go looking for that "awakening" about the value of my sight. But the experience arrived in my life and nudged me towards a greater appreciation of its importance.

Other experiences have awakened me to the joys of the moment as well. My mother's massive stroke. The break-up of my first marriage. Single motherhood. The death of my husband.

I've lived through four custody fights and the financial Armageddon that resulted, and I've struggled with a range of family issues that have left me drained and discouraged.

The list goes on for an interesting three decades and at the end of it all, what I really know for sure is that every time I have suffered a loss, a hurt, a disappointment or a perceptive failure, I have been gifted with the compensation of an amazing, heart-felt awakening. Health is crucial. Love is precious. I am resilient. Children are miracles. Life is fleeting. I am worthy. The universe is mysterious. And, somehow, God always provides.

These are all statements that for many years I believed on an intellectual level, more or less. I knew it was important to be appreciative, I knew I was a survivor. But what my awakenings have done for me, personally, was to take the wisdom of my experience out of my head and write it into the DNA of my heart.

It's one thing to know that sight is important. It's a totally different issue to feel the crushing worry that at 21 years old you will never drive a car again if you cannot pass a vision test, and that experimental surgery is your only hope. The relief of a successful operation is stratospheric in its impact.

It's one thing to know that strokes limit mobility. It's a totally different knowledge to watch your highly independent mother inch her way across a busy street as cars threaten her life and people stop and stare. The gift of compassion that results is love at its most elemental.

The list goes steadily on.

It's one thing to understand that half of all marriages end in divorce and that divorce means poverty for many single families. It's another thing entirely to quietly forego dinner because you want your children to be strong for their tests tomorrow. The appreciation for a solid meal ever after is exquisite.

It's one thing to understand, on an intellectual level, that we are all going to die. It's a totally different experience to watch someone you love take their very last breath. The determination to strive for fullness in the life remaining to you is humbling.

It's one thing to believe we have empathy for a widowed mother of two young children. It's a totally different experience to actually BE that mother and feel the dreams of a happy family life evaporate in the heart-breaking memory of a morphine injection.

Compassion for others in their most profoundly difficult moments is not an intellectual exercise. Its birth requires the understanding of a caring heart and the commitment of a willing soul.

It is a fragile exercise. And it requires us to be awake to who we are and to be open to the possibilities for a better way of being in the world.

We are seeing this play out at the international level now as more people become conscious of something loosely termed the global awakening movement. This is a growing collaboration of people focused on helping others live more empowered, successful and fulfilling lives by helping them overcome the beliefs and behaviours that are holding them hostage.

It's about spreading awareness of the fact that change is possible and dreams do come true. If every one of us were to live our lives to our fullest potential, so the theory goes, then the Earth would be transmuted.

We would shift from a hostile, war-torn territory peopled by angry and frustrated human beings to a peace-loving planet brimming with hope.

Who knows where this will all lead? But it's interesting that every awakening each of us experiences provides an opening through which we can access a bigger version of ourselves. And as we grow, learn and develop, we affect everyone around us.

More to the point, as we awaken, we allow the light of more understanding to shine on the world we live in. It is that light that will keep us warm and help show the way to ever greater experiences and opportunities

And once we are awake, we can't go back to sleep. We can still, however, dare to dream.

Winter's Woe

A True Story

Winter has become something of an endurance test for me in recent decades and I blame my years as a pre-schooler in Dryden, Ontario, for my reluctance to put myself within reach of the arctic blessing of the winter wind.

Dryden is a special place for me, almost magical in its grip on my memory, and although I remember endless summer days spent mostly on my tricycle, I also remember peering out into the coldest night on record with my tongue stuck to the handle of our back screen door.

I'm sure it couldn't be helped.

I was a curious child, ever alert to new possibilities. If I'm not mistaken, it was one of the many nights when I, my sister and several of our cousins were heading off for an evening of skating at an outdoor rink located several blocks away. Preparations were endless as we stuffed ourselves into long johns, extra socks, snow suits and woolen mittens.

Once I was tightly trussed and perspiring greatly I was expected to stand quietly and wait for the others. This was next to impossible. From beyond the kitchen window I could see the snow glittering in a pool of light cast by a nearby streetlight. It looked like diamonds had been sprinkled all over our front yard. What if they were real?

One of the adults opened the sturdy inside door that kept out most of the cold, most of the time, and I gratefully began to cool off. I was at the front of the line, eager to roll out into that exciting black night. Maybe we would see those pretty shimmers of coloured light in the sky that my parents called the Northern Lights! Maybe we would see a snowplow! I leaned against the screen door.

"Stay inside, Suzie, it's not time yet," my mother said. I don't remember the exact flicker of intellect that spurred me into deciding it would be a good idea to lick the door handle while I waited for the signal to press forward but I knew almost immediately that it was a bad idea.

"OK Suzie let's go!"

It is very difficult to tell someone your tongue has glued itself to frozen metal. I pulled. It hurt. I cried. Adults frowned. The nattering of happy children behind me turned my panic into terror. Eventually an impatient parent determined the cause of the problem and dribbled warm water onto the handle's surface. My mouth tasted like metallic blood but I was free!

I have repeatedly warned my own children to refrain from making the same mistake I did and fortunately none of them have been so inclined. Instead they look at me in exasperation and say "Mom, that would be *stupid*." Naturally I say nothing in response. Sometimes there is dignity in silence.

Hold Your Nose – Jump

Musings on a Last Date

A True Story

We all know the life of a single mother is full of challenges and disappointments and as the self-employed mother of a lively six-year-old, I'd had enough. It was the endless winter of 1993 and I'd been fighting fatigue, bill collectors, my ex-husband AND the clock-- for years. I needed some goodness in my life.

Actually, I needed a miracle and I arrived at my home office late one afternoon after an especially tough day to find it: my high school sweetheart had left a message on my voice mail wanting "to shoot the breeze," as he put it.

I felt a shock of delight.

I had last bumped into Steve by chance some years earlier when both of us were married to our first spouses and the puppy love that had marked our year of high-school hand-holding had become a distant memory. We had said hello, exchanged our news and gone on with our lives.

As time passed we both started our families and ended our marriages. We were light years removed from the turbulence of high school life in London, Ontario. But thinking back to the romance of young love, and hoping the young girl he had so ardently cared about might still be hiding in the woman I had become, Steve tracked down my phone number and gave me a call.

We set a date for dinner. The evening could not arrive soon enough and I was light-hearted and cheerful when he arrived with flowers and a shy smile.

We had the worst date ever.

The playful and unconventional high-school troublemaker I had fallen in love with at 15 had become stiff and starchy, highly educated and a little bit dull.

From Steve's perspective, I was no prize either. The high-achieving sprite he'd once known was now awash in struggle, submerged in a misery of doubt and caution.

Nothing was said at the time, but we agreed to go out again. And again. And one more time. I decided our next date would be our last.

Steve arrived promptly on time and I walked resolutely out my front door to his waiting car. I was planning to develop a bad headache and then go home early to watch "Little House on the Prairie" reruns in my fuzzy slippers and sweat suit.

But Fate had other plans.

We headed off to a noisy roadhouse restaurant for a last meal of beer, wings, nachos and endurance. Several hours went by before I realized I was supposed to be home on my couch with an imaginary migraine. Steve and I talked and joked, and even held hands for one brief second. He kissed me on the cheek.

Many more wonderful times followed and eventually we married, uniting our three children in the artistic bond of a step-family; we created two more little lives together and bought a dog. Two dogs. We laughed and loved, dreamed and planned. There was struggle and persistence in our fairy tale romance but we moved forward together, ever curious about what was going to happen next. We often joked about how lucky we were that our "last date" had turned out so well.

After 14 dynamic years of life together, Steve was diagnosed with advanced stomach cancer. Treatment was pointless; he was given mere months to live. At first I sobbed uncontrollably and then, as the rigors of providing at-home care for a terminally ill spouse grew, there was no time for self-pity or reflection. His pain was unrelenting. We suffered and endured. Our children did not dare cry.

Days before Steve passed away, he was admitted into the compassionate kindness of the West Island Palliative Care Centre in Pointe-Claire, Quebec. His pain was finally put to rest and we squarely faced the end of his life and all that might come thereafter for each of us.

The night before he slipped into a coma, I boosted his frail body into a wheelchair and pushed him down the hall to the calm little dining room kept for the Centre's residents and their families. Staff lit candles for our table and we held hands securely, allowing our grief to accompany the last meal I would ever attempt to eat at my husband's side.

"I guess there really is a last date," Steve said.

I nodded my head and looked lovingly through endless tears at the perfect green eyes that had steadied me so often during the past 14 years. Although we'd passed thousands of hours in comfortable conversation there was still so much I wanted to tell him, so much I wanted to explore at his side. "Our last date was perfect," he said.

I kissed him on the cheek.

The next day, he slipped into a restful coma and the day after that he slipped into whatever world waits beyond the veil of this life. He was a 49-year-old father of five children and he had been sick for only three months; oceans of grief pummeled my heart.

The experience of my husband's passing has given me surprising gifts, however. Although there is much to regret in the early death of someone who is loved, there is grace as well, and it peeks out occasionally between the tears and sorrow to give a hint of comfort.

Throughout our journey together, Steve and I had the blessing of knowing we had come dangerously close to missing the chance to become partners in the astonishing adventure of Life – the messy, hold-your-nose-and-jump tangle of doubt and hope that anyone with a dash of gumption gets enmeshed within as they go about their daily routine.

I'm awfully glad our first "last date" worked out. And I'm grateful that our last "last date" brought us full circle, to an end that was also a beginning, painful though that has been. There are no promises in life. But hidden in among the thorns of unexpected misery, there are compensations.

I think Steve would have liked that idea.

Of Pets and Procreation

A True Story

Children are sweet creatures but somewhat wily when it comes to pet ownership and when my own kids launched their Puppy Campaign a few years ago there was only one possible response: No.

"But Mom we *need* a dog," came the anguished rebuttal.

And they probably did.

My children's father had died a few months earlier, while we were all still recovering from the demise of our beloved chocolate lab, Zeppy. The year before that, we had sadly faced the passing of my own wonderful father. The business of death was weighing on all of us and the thought of a puppy prancing around our ankles had some appeal.

But my husband's death had brought many new responsibilities for me: I had moved us back to Ontario from Montreal and begun the challenging work of re-launching my business on a solo footing. Another dog?

"No," I said.

"Please Mummy, just a little one."

"NO."

"Wouldn't you love another dog?"

"No!"

Well, yes.

Zeppy had been my constant friend, a beautiful and playful charmer whose boundless love had accompanied me through 13 eventful years. He had sniffed at grass, trees and dirty socks until his hips gave out and his pain became more than I could endure. But I couldn't bear the thought of losing yet another best friend.

"A cat then."

"No, silly, Mummy doesn't like cats."

"I'm allergic," I said.

"Please Mummy, just one cat?"

Two pairs of perfect blue eyes pleaded up at me.

"How about a nice house plant?" I said.

Phil the Philodendron and Brancher the Palm Bush moved into our house and did not die.

But the quest for a pet continued. A gecko, a hamster and a bunny were vetoed – repeatedly – and I had finally forbidden all talk of a new pet.

I was beginning to think I had actually won the day when the revolution took a more sinister turn. I was busy scraping gum out of the bottom of a coffee cup one perfect summer Saturday when my son roared into the kitchen and asked for a jar with holes in the lid.

"How cute," I thought.

I showed him the jar supply, punched some holes in a lid and returned to my Saturday routine. Hours later I noticed seven large jars lined up along the back of the kitchen counter. They looked nice sitting there, loaded with grass, leaves and dirt.

But there were rather a lot of them.

"What's in there?" I asked.

My son grinned.

"Slugs and SNAILS!"

They seemed harmless enough and it appeared that resistance was futile so the next day we bought a tank and filled it with more grass and dirt. The critters could stay if the kids looked after them – and ensured they had zero impact on my life.

My son fed the snails faithfully for weeks, even after the slugs had mysteriously disappeared, and he cleaned their lair without grumbling. One crisp October morning, we noticed the inside of the tank was festooned with hundreds of baby snails.

I felt faint.

Cleaning the tank was out of the question – we might inadvertently kill some of the babies. Weeks went by and the tank became a foul monument to pet ownership; the colony moved into the garden without a fight.

I was so relieved to be rid of the snails that I foolishly agreed to replace them with fish – "as long as they have zero impact on my life," I warned.

Four fish moved into a squeaky clean tank and expired one by one. Calls were made to the fish store. Remedies were attempted. Replacement fish were purchased. The "zero impact" concept was working poorly and after many months of fish replacement I put my foot down.

"When Swimmy and Swummy are gone there will be, NO more fish," I declared.

We were running late one morning and eager to leave for the day when we caught Swummy chomping on poor Swimmy's fins. Outraged, I filled a large bowl with water and put Swummy in the clink.

"Bad fish," I said. "I'll deal with you later." We returned home that evening to find Swummy lying motionless on the kitchen floor, a tragic suicide, presumably related to a failed effort to finish his snack.

Now down to one lone fish I started to relax. One fish is not such a big deal, I thought.

Relaxation is dangerous in our house, however, and one morning I noticed two tiny fish darting around the tank.

"Look Mummy, Swimmy had babies!" my daughter cooed.

"Impossible" I snarled. "That Mother has been alone in the tank for three months."

Nevertheless the babies existed and they were kind of cute. We segregated them for their own protection and they are still scooting around the tank, somewhat larger now, but alive nonetheless.

Although my children seem mollified, printouts about the care and ownership of turtles have started appearing on my placemat with alarming regularity.

It occurs to me that the circle of life and death, love and pets is endless and eternal, one of those issues generations of parents have been confronting since children first appeared on the planet. I'm not crazy about the idea of a turtle, although the inevitable babies might be sweet. And I'm still not sold on the idea of a dog, the animal, my children really want to welcome.

"You need a boyfriend," my son said to me the other day.

"WHAT?" I said. I am just starting to feel I've got this widow business figured out and I still like that "zero impact" idea. A boyfriend might be a time consuming project, one I'm not quite ready to manage.

"Why on Earth do you want me to get a boyfriend?" I asked.

My son looked nonchalantly up at the ceiling and shrugged.

"Sometimes men like dogs," he said.

I looked at my boy, surging bravely towards manhood and nodded my head.

"I guess the right one would have to," I said.

The Meaning of Life

A True Story

It's the day before summer camp begins and I have suddenly realized that I have figured out the true meaning of life. I wasn't actually working on the project, truth be told. But somehow the exhausting effort of gathering and labeling the tangle of equipment that litters my living room floor has given me insights I would never have summoned otherwise.

It's a colorful scene, if intimidating. Bright yellow life jackets mingle with orange tubes of sunscreen and green cans of bug spray. Fat puffy sleeping bags (one red, one blue) mixed in with a snuggle toy, a yoyo and a deck of cards. There are books, water bottles, safety whistles and a large scramble of T-shirts, swim suits and beach towels that are, apparently, babyish.

Last year's paddles are present and accounted for but they're too short now, and my son has found his father's old rain jacket, which is way too big for a 12-year-old; he is taking it anyway. There was a list at one point and naturally it has been lost in the excitement and confusion of packing. I'm convinced we've forgotten something important and I'm thinking it's time for a large gin and tonic.

Everywhere I look I see the confusing signs of the old mingled in with the new, items that are too big co-existing brightly with those that are too small. In a few hours we will stuff it all into hockey bags and try and get some sleep.

My children will no doubt be dreaming tonight of canoe trips, camp fires and sing-songs. They'll be looking forward to endless tether ball competitions and the joyful release of swimming in a sandy lake. They'll drift off to sleep in a cool northern cabin and then awaken the next morning to do it all again.

I can't wait.

Much as I feel privileged to be the sole parent of two amazing and wonderful children, I find myself crawling to their annual two-week trip to summer camp with little more than a flimsy grip on my positive attitude. I'm getting used to the load of responsibility I inherited upon the death of my husband three years ago but I still need a break every now and then. Like other parents in my situation, my days are more about crisis management than calm proficiency.

Aside from homework, meals, groceries and garbage, I earn the income, pay the bills, weed the garden and make sure that we don't run out of important staples like dill pickles and raspberry jam. I set the rules, adjudicate disputes and mete out justice as required. I even walk the dog I insisted we get after my children gave up asking for one.

In fact, I think I need my children's summer camp even more than they do.

While they are tramping through the bush swatting mosquitoes and learning how to use a compass, I will be working quietly away at my desk and completing every single thing on my daily task list. Then I'll go out into my garden and hum quietly to myself. No one will complain about the working or the humming.

While my kids are learning key skills like the J-Stroke and how to climb back into an upset canoe, I will be off on a long bike ride along paths I haven't yet explored. While they are eating burned marshmallows and singing complicated camp songs, I will curl up in front of a movie that will be much too serious, dramatic or romantic for children.

I will eat cheese and crackers for dinner, or maybe ice cream and dark chocolate, and I will end my summer camp holiday feeling refreshed, recharged and resilient.

I will be desperate to see my kids again.

My children, meanwhile, will probably be ready to come home as well. They will have been running, playing, socializing and learning for two solid weeks without benefit of computer games or iPod downloads.

They will have forgotten all about the tired mother who wants to know if they've done their laundry, and they will have replaced her with the cheerful Mother who loves to tease.

When they get off that bus after two weeks in the sun, they will be tanned and glowing, scratched and grubby, and full of wonderful stories they just can't wait to tell me. I will hang on every word.

When September arrives, far too quickly, I will pack them off to school with honest regret.

But I'll have the elusive meaning of life to steady me this year. Because what I learned from that pile of unruly camp supplies on the living room floor is that life centres almost entirely around balance.

Jumbled in with the new, the oversized and the cautionary are the old, the way-too-small and the frivolous.

Exhaustion pairs with rejuvenation, playing with learning, society with isolation. As a parent I think I had forgotten the fact that life balances out eventually, with our help or without.

Crazy and hectic as my life is most of the time now, I realize there will come a day – and probably not long from now – when I will miss the chaos of raising children, the crisis of losing lists. And there is balance in that too.

But for now, we will pack everything neatly into those two waiting hockey bags and enjoy our last busy evening together before the wheel turns and we head off onto the detour from our daily life that summer camp offers.

Sometime before my children tuck into bed, I will slip sit outside and sit on my front porch to gather my resources for that excited trip tomorrow to the camp bus stop. I will sip my gin and think about what I'm going to do on my summer holiday. And I will feel grateful for chaos and the order it invites.

Novelissimo

A True Story

My son looked up at me from his post at the kitchen table, his blue eyes staring at me reproachfully from behind a spoonful of Cheerios.

"Mum?" he asked sternly, stretching the word out so it bowed in the middle and ended on a higher pitch.

"What?" I said. I was on the defensive and emotionally more than a little on the run.

He was only 12 years old but he had the stance of a lawyer who might one day adopt a nickname like "Crush" or "Pitbull." While my two daughters might gracefully let me squirm away from an uncomfortable question, my son never will and I owe him a debt of gratitude for pushing me on the issue we were discussing at the time.

"I *asked* you when you were going to get your book published," he said with a noble courtroom flourish.

Truth to tell I had pretty much given up on the project. I had started writing a novel when the little league lawyer in question was no more than a twinkle in his father's eye. Twelve years of raising five children, supporting my spouse in his career, finding time to do a little freelance work and walking a father, a dog and finally the spouse himself to their appointment with the Other Side of Life...it had all quenched much of my earlier enthusiasm.

I had tackled the job of replacing my husband's income with determination but I was tired. I was lonely. I was discouraged. And I didn't think I had any time or energy available to continue working on my novel.

Like many other would-be novelists, I have wanted to become a published author since I was all of about eight years old. I used to climb into the backyard apple tree clutching a writing pad and a stubby HB pencil and scribble endlessly between doses of daydreaming and mouthfuls of Macintosh.

In high school I wrote soulful and self-centred poetry about the anguish of young love and the confusion of growing up. In university, I wrote for my student newspaper.

As time went on, I realized that creative writing was unlikely to generate the income necessary to support myself, let alone a family. So I turned to jobs that would at least let me write: Journalism. Marketing, Government communications, Public Relations.

I felt grateful to be able to make my way in the world with language as my stock in trade. I took courses and found writing mentors to emulate. But there was a wayward part of me that kept thinking, "But I *really* want to write fiction!"

A few years into my second marriage my husband confronted me on the topic.

"It's something you've always wanted to do," he said. "What's stopping you?" I had a million reasons not to do it – self-doubt, anxiety and the fear of not being good enough led the list. But they all dissolved in the face of that question. Actually, nothing was actually *stopping* me.

Other than me.

So I began the fun and endless task of creating a story. I had no clue what I was doing or how one was supposed to write a novel. I just jumped in and wrote. I wrote a story about a woman who faced challenge and disappointment but who gathered up her courage and turned a dream into a reality.

By the time my husband drifted off into his final slumber I had managed to wrestle myself into completing a final draft. But I had a heartful of tears, two children to raise and a business to run. My novel seemed trivial, somehow, in the face of eternity, and yet more important than ever.

We don't know how much time we have left on this planet to make our mark and I agonized over my own future. What if I died before seeing if my manuscript could be turned into a real book someday? What if my novel actually *could* become a published work? How would I ever know if I didn't try?

But what if my children went hungry because their mother couldn't make a successful living as a freelancer?

Practicality very slowly won over and I quietly began neglecting the effort to find an agent.

By the time of my son's inquisition I was manfully ignoring the irritating voice in the back of my head that wanted me to pursue my dream.

"I don't know," I said.

My son chewed thoughtfully and then took another mouthful of cereal. After a moment he put his spoon down and looked at me wisely.

"You're always telling us kids that we should never give up," he said. "How can we do that if you don't show us how?"

His words curdled in my heart.

How indeed? And then this:

You can do it, Mum! Pleeeease?"

And so I did.

Manor House Books published "Shades of Teale" at the end of November and all three of my children are proud of their mother in a way I could never have imagined. It has been a long journey and I've learned much. But it appears there's more to come. My son, now 13 and still a fan of Cheerios, feels I've really only just started this novelist business and there is much more to be done on the topic.

"So when is your book going to be a best-seller?" he asked the other day.

I groaned.

"I think we might have to give that one a little more time," I said.

My son raised an eyebrow and looked at me sceptically.

"Mum?"

Powder Puff in Peril

A Single Mom Tackles Snowboarding

A True Story

As the self-employed widowed mom of three great kids I don't tend to fill my life with wild adventure but when my two youngest children suggested we go snowboarding one day I gave the idea an immediate thumbs up.

A few hours spent swinging up and down Blue Mountain on a snowboard would burn hundreds of calories, I figured -- probably way more than skiing – and what middle aged woman doesn't want to burn a few more calories?

What's more, this could turn into something fun we could do together as my kids journeyed through those parent-o-phobic teenage years that lay just beyond the next school dance.

It didn't occur to me that snowboarding might be easier said than done until well after the snowboard rental people had determined that we were newbies par excellence.

Did we know where to rendezvous for our lesson, the nice ski pro asked? He was young and cute and he looked fit and healthy, almost as if he spent his whole life outside.

It occurred to me that there just might be a nice, single 55-year-old man out there in snow-board land, one who would look at my technique with huge appreciation and ask me out for a drink. Maybe we would swap stories about our travels and goals, and agree to go out for dinner in a nice romantic restaurant (no kids allowed). Maybe he might even like disorderly dogs and messy houses. The possibilities were intriguing.

"Lesson?" I asked. "Oh we don't need lessons!"

The young man looked at me with respect but said nothing. I marched my children emphatically out to the lift lines.

My daughter stared up at the mountain and pointed at a snowboarder who was gliding gracefully down the pristine flank of snow.

"Let's try that hill Mum," she said.

I smiled. My 11-year-old daughter is blessed with a love of adventure that I no longer embrace. She knows there are moguls in life but that hasn't discouraged her from living large.

"Oh Sweetie, I don't think we should start on a *big* hill," I said soothingly. "We've never done this before and we'll want to have a practice run first." I was worried that my children might get hurt.

A dozen more boarders flew by us as we made our way, a little awkwardly, over to the baby hill. We breezed up the gentle incline standing comfortably on a rubber lift mat. I patted my hat to make sure my hair wasn't escaping in messy tendrils. People might be watching.

Snowboarders whizzed by with practiced ease and I couldn't wait to join them. It looked like so much fun!

I slid off the lift mat at the top of the hill and buckled my second foot into the snowboard. My children headed off down the hill and I watched them affectionately. They would get the hang of it.

I knew I was in trouble the second I started moving.

With my feet locked in place at such a bizarre angle I was completely incapable of balancing. Sliding oddly down the hill with my arms flailing, I progressed approximately two metres before my rear end hit the snow. A little embarrassed, I stood up with great difficulty and tried again, this time managing to progress a good 12 centimetres before I caught an edge and flipped over. I looked around and waved gamely at my children who were by then half way up the hill, eager for their second run.

I wobbled to my feet. This time I swung immediately around and started sliding uncontrollably down the hill backwards with my bottom pointing skyward and my ski mitts clawing uselessly at the hard packed snow of the bunny hill. There were three-year-olds all over the place and every single one of them was in my way. What were parents thinking, bringing little children out into such a dangerous place?! I careened out of control and planted my knees in the snow just seconds before executing a perfect face plant.

"Are you OK?" my daughter asked from somewhere above me

I grinned up at her, wincing at the pain in my knees.

"Great," I said. "Are you having fun?"

"Sort of," she said.

"Good!" I croaked. This snowboarding business was not nearly as enjoyable as it had looked.

My daughter zoomed off and I refocused on survival.

The next half hour was painful and awkward. There were children everywhere and every adult on the hill seemed to be glaring viciously in my direction.

When I arrived at the bottom of the hill I was breathing heavily and sweating profusely.

Enough was enough. Any single male of eligible age had undoubtedly enjoyed the comedy show I had put on but was unlikely to feel safe in a bar with me ("What if she falls over AGAIN?!" I could hear Mr. Right whispering in horror to his best friend). This had not been my finest moment and I was bruised, exhausted, embarrassed and finished with this idea of snowboarding as a fun way to spend time.

My children reappeared at the bottom of Bunny Mountain and I limped back to the rental shack to exchange our snowboards for proper skis.

"Thank goodness," my daughter said. I brightened.

"Oh, did you find it hard?" I asked with relief.

"No," she said, squeezing my arm gently and flashing a warm and caring smile up at me. "But you did."

My Father's Legacy

A True Story

My sister and I stared down at the neatly arranged collection of items our step-mother had placed on the floor of my father's workshop and we took a deep breath. Lynda had asked us to finish the task of dividing up the markers of a life well-lived, and the project rang of finality in a way Dad's funeral five years earlier had not.

Crystal tumblers that had held Dad's beloved pre-dinner scotch rested peacefully beside the little silver bucket that had contained the ice necessary for cooling it. A set of Royal Doulton dishes sat parked in a cardboard box just behind a tall silver pitcher that had once stood resplendent and full of flowers in the middle of our dining room table.

The workshop was a lonely place that dull spring afternoon, and it rang of a desolation the sparkling souvenirs we were about to inherit could not dispel. The mute colony of Dad's belongings lay stretched out on a white sheet that did nothing to warm the cold concrete underneath. A pile of newspapers sat waiting to wrap the fragile memories of Dad's life, so they could survive the journey to their new homes intact. The room was cold. When Dad was alive, his workshop had been a vibrant place full of tools and machinery. Boxes of nails and screws had been stored neatly on his workbench and countless pieces of wood had been filed by shape and type on the sturdy shelves he had built to house them.

The heavenly smell of sawdust had permeated the air and the atmosphere had been cheerful and orderly. Dad had

had a passion for wood and he had spent his life avidly learning its mysteries. He owned the right tool for every woodly task, and he had an impressive collection of sandpaper. He had patiently coached me through my first furniture refinishing project, a dilapidated old sideboard I had picked up at a garage sale. He was a wonderful teacher. Dad taught me that there are no shortcuts in refinishing furniture. Each step in the process is time consuming and laborious. But there is a Zen to the work, a deliberate and almost meditative rhythm that is soothing and satisfying. Dad had discovered this peace early in his life and he had passed it along to both my sister and me.

Upon Dad's death the contents of his workshop passed into my sister's keeping and his library made its way to me. Dad had amassed hundreds of books on every topic imaginable, and he had developed a compassionate understanding of the intricate grain of human life. He knew how each step in the process of walking into our full humanity takes time and effort, and this approach enlightened his parenting beautifully: he had coaxed the best out of my sister and I much as he had coaxed beauty from non-descript scraps of wood.

Somehow he knew the grain of our being, the potential hidden within, the possibilities we each contained that just needed to be freed into reality with the careful carving wrought by a thoughtful question, an insightful comment, or an eyebrow raised at a pertinent moment. He saw into the stolid block of us and knew there was something else within, something fine and noble and beautiful; something greater than we thought we ever could become. As a craftsman, he carried out his steady work with care and wisdom, tenderness and confidence. One day we emerged, fully formed and vibrant, ready for Life to complete the work he had so faithfully begun.

The removal of the books from our former home had made little difference to Dad's workroom — they had sat on bookshelves in other rooms — but the absence of his tools turned his workshop into a dismal place, no longer warmed by his cheerful energy. Despite the treasures we were about to claim, the room itself felt empty of Dad now.

"Where do we start?" my sister asked.

We glanced at the crystal vases and glass bowls, the handcrafted wooden boxes and the cherished family pictures. And we looked beyond the glitter to the grit of Dad's life: a car battery charger, a bicycle pump, a cycling helmet, a well-worn tool belt. By what criteria would we select or reject the remnants of a life, especially when the significance of that life was marked by the hearts it strengthened, rather than the objects it collected?

Our step-mother wisely stepped aside while we deliberated. Lynda had gradually rebuilt her life after the debilitating experience of nursing our father through a cancer death. She had gradually eased herself onto a new path and over time she had developed a growing fondness for a family friend, a kind man who had lost his own wife shortly after Dad had passed away. Lynda was ready to move on with her life now.

Would we ever do the same?

Debbie and I sat cross-legged on the concrete floor and surveyed the scene around us, two middle-aged women privy to each other's past in the way only siblings can be. No-one else would remember the secrets we had whispered to each other in a shared bedroom in the small Northern Ontario house of our childhood, or the sailing adventures that had tacked us across our teenage years. We had both reluctantly pushed a green and white electric lawnmower across the big lawns of our home in London, Ontario, and we remembered, with fondness, the peppy but failing blue sports car Debbie had driven off to university. We were rooted together in a common soil, one that was drifting away into a quiet past with the slow winds of time.

But our lives were not just comprised of sequential events that had simply "occurred." They were also the tumultuous streams of vital experiences that had touched us deeply and affected us intensely. There had been the excited Christmas mornings spent in our pyjamas as we waited to open the annual gift of socks, and the long camping trips that took us hundreds of miles from home. Dad was fond of camping, and after a long day spent in the car we'd tumble out on restless legs and scramble through the underbrush looking for tinder. Dad would set up the tent with a minimum of cussing and Mom would organize a meal of pork and beans or spaghetti that we would cheerfully consume in Nature's dining room.

After dinner we'd sit around the campfire and try to out-maneuver the pungent and ever-shifting camp smoke while we listened to choruses of crickets and frogs.

Sometime before we became too drowsy to notice, Dad would pull out his knife and a piece of wood he'd found and start uncovering the arrowhead or ankh hidden within. He'd scrape away at the fibres of wood while we grew cool and sleepy in the half light of the fire. Dad worked slowly and intentionally, one careful curl of wood coming away after another, until the final shape emerged. Later, Dad would smile modestly at his work and gently feed the shavings he had created to the fire – he hated leaving a mess behind. We owed it to our father now to ensure the last pieces of his life were tidied into new usefulness, and we began our deliberations with a great deal of good will.

We waded our way through family photographs and Royal Doulton dishes, silver vases and wooden boxes. There was artwork to divide and hand-made toast tongs to admire. Hours of discussion and negotiation were enlightened by funny stories and fond memories.

We sanded down the years like Dad had sanded down his precious wood, revelling in the way the grain began to surface, stopping in surprise as an unexpected insight came to light, or an unremembered story surfaced for re-evaluation. Sometimes we would apply a conclusion to those insights, a conclusion that would sit like a coat of varathane on raw wood, protecting the grain and sealing in new lustre for another day.

That empty workroom became a more cheerful place for a while, warmed by the memories of the amazing man our father was, the wonderful gifts of compassion and kind-heartedness he had passed along to us and others, the lessons of diligence and patience he had imparted.

When we pulled our cars out of the driveway of the house that had once been our home the next day, we carried valuable cargo and beautiful treasures; symbols of our father's life. Gratitude is a kind companion and we were both touched by our final communion with our father's gifts. He was a willing carpenter in the construction of our lives and he had helped each of us find and live in alignment with the grains of our own existence.

It occurs to me now that this diligent work is craftsmanship in its finest form. Dad may have left this world for whatever lies beyond the veil of this life. But his legacy lives on.

The Sedona Experience:

Psychic Woo and Serenity

A Travel Story

Gazing out at the majestic red rocks around Sedona, Arizona, it's possible to imagine a mystical wind blowing through the streets of this desert town. And judging by the number of businesses here that are focused on intuitive and spiritual practices, that just might be the case.

Spiritual awakening is a big focus of life in this city of 11,000: it's easy to find your way to a psychic or Tarot Card reading, but you can also arrange for everything from a past life regression to a Shamangelic Healing. This is a town where crystal and hypno-therapists mingle with astrologers and Reiki masters. You can find opportunities to balance your chakras or photograph your aura. You can clear your Akashic Records, visit a sweat lodge, connect to your higher purpose or open your third eye.

Walk along Sedona's main streets and you'll find retail outlets offering cowboy boots and western clothing resting comfortably beside stores that carry gemstones, tarot cards, angelic gift items and feng shui supplies.

A total of 113 intuitive, metaphysical and/or spiritually-based businesses and services are listed with the Sedona Chamber of Commerce, a substantial number given the fact that this is a city with fewer than 11,000 residents. The city's most recent Visitor's Survey found that 15% of all visitors came for Spiritual and Metaphysical purposes, while 20% came to visit a "Vortex" or take a "Vortex Tour"

There are hundreds of businesses in Sedona offering products and services that have no bearing on spiritual exploration in Sedona at all, of course. But as a tourist destination for spiritual seekers, this town just can't be beat.

Elaine Edelson is an empath and astro-intuitive channel who lives and works in the village of Oak Creek on the outskirts of Sedona. She is a straightforward woman who comes across as practical, grounded and realistic about the challenges of living intuitively in a world where sceptics abound.

"My first visit to Sedona more than 25 years ago was one of the most profound experiences of my life," she says.

"Everything just opened for me," she notes. "I felt immediately at home, completely grounded in my body and totally aligned with my purpose in life."

In 2002, after many more visits, Edelson and her family decided to leave Los Angeles and relocate to Sedona.

"It's quiet here for me," she says. "I can think my own thoughts easily. As an empath, I find the barrage of information, sights, sounds and stressors that come at me in big cities can be overwhelming.

"My focus in life now is on helping people feel empowered to make conscious choices that lead to wealth, health, passion and purpose in this lifetime," she says. "It's the ideal amalgamation of the practical and the spiritual.

"People coming to seek the 'Sedona Experience' are looking to find their message, to be guided," she adds.

"But as my husband says, don't look for it — let it find you, because when you're 'looking for it,' you're in your head, rather than in your heart."

Edelson notes that she does a lot of hiking in Sedona and she often bumps into visitors asking for directions to one of the area's famous vortices.

"I'll just smile and point to their heart," she says.

According to New Age philosophy, there are numerous places on Earth where special energies called vortices are thought to facilitate prayer, healing, meditation and a connection to God.

Similar energy centres have apparently been identified in Stonehenge, England, Machu Picchu, Peru, and in the region where the Great Pyramids of Egypt stand sentinel over desert expanses. According to New Age theory, grid lines deep inside the Earth link these ancient sites with sources of cosmic energy inside the planet to create a heightened energy field.

The four most commonly identified Vortexes in Sedona are at:

Airport Mesa (relatively close to the Uptown area of Sedona);

Bell Rock (adjacent to the Village of Oak Creek)

Boynton Canyon (located in West Sedona)

Cathedral Rock (on Lower Red Rock Loop Road)

Numerous companies offer guided visits by jeep for those interested in experiencing the energy of a Vortex. And although some visitors say they don't feel any different at a vortex than anywhere else, it's said that a vortex can heighten a person's consciousness and strengthen their sense of purpose. Feelings of exhilaration or intense self-reflection might be expected. Whether or not these claims are true, there is no doubt that the scenery is stunning.

Sedona is surrounded by the 1.8 million-acre Coconino National Forest and the beautiful magic of the desert is everywhere, from the abundant and majestic rock formations rising up above the desert floor to the thousands of cacti keeping vigil by darkness and daylight.

Karolyn Blume is an attorney from Arlington, Virginia, who specializes in conflict resolution. She took two jeep/hiking tours while in Sedona recently and found that "the tours are really only as good as the leaders on the tour." While she raved about the natural beauty of the Sedona area, she found that the trip she took up a rise called Mystic Vista was particularly moving.

"I don't know anything about 'psychic woo,' "she says, "but there really was something there. It made the hairs on the back of my neck stand up."

Blume's job requires her to work often with people who are angry and hostile, and she says that bringing them to peaceful and collaborative agreements can be stressful.

"I meditate sometimes but I don't usually get very far," she adds. "By the third breath I'm thinking about my 'To do' list and thinking about who I have to call."

"I felt much more open on Mystic Rise, though, and I ended up having a couple of personal breakthroughs while I was there," she notes. "What was it about Sedona that made that happen? I can't even guess."

Blume says she loves the outdoors and she had been attracted to Sedona originally because of what she'd heard about its natural beauty."

"It's one of the most naturally beautiful places I've ever seen," she says.

"There's a certain tranquility or serenity about Sedona and I think if you're quiet it really affects you. I just went out and looked at the mountains and got a really serene feeling about it all. For me that's interesting because I don't usually feel serene. There really was a calm presence in Sedona," she adds. "It really affected me."

Spiritual Tourism

A new twist on an old idea

A Travel Story

The stately mountains of western Canada look serenely down on the shimmering turquoise water of Emerald Lake in Field, British Columbia, and the air is cool and clean. A light rain is falling but I and the 18 other people linked together in canoes in the middle of the lake are motionless and silent. We're all meditating peacefully and listening for the messages we were called to this space to receive.

By the standards of "normal" with which I was raised, this is an odd thing to be doing.

What's more, the messages we await will not be broadcast from speakers hidden in the pristine forest circling the lake, but rather they are expected to emerge gently, if inaudibly, from deep within the hearts of each one of us. I have a vague notion that my mother and others of her generation would find this exercise something of a waste of time, but I'm here and I'm curious: what am I supposed to get?

The folks joining me on this excursion are sitting more or less comfortably in the bottom of their wet canoes and they're a uniformly cheerful bunch. We've come from towns and cities across North America to gather with tour leader Daniel Gutierrez in what we understand to be a spiritually significant location. Although most of us have never met face-to-face before, we seek to share a philosophy that sees abundance in all things as a state of being, as well as a birthright.

This "message" idea takes a little getting used to, however.

Gutierrez is a Los Angeles-based international business consultant, author and motivational speaker. He has coached each member of our group on issues relating to the spiritual nature of abundance, either one-on-one or as part of a daily group telephone coaching call. His motto of "Go Within or Go Without" reflects his belief that a person's connection to their Creator determines their ability to reveal the desires of their heart.

Gutierrez says a visit to Emerald Lake on a stormy day a year ago was the catalyst for this extraordinary gathering. He and a friend watched the lake and waited until the rain stopped, and then they paddled a canoe to the middle of the lake for messages of their own.

"I was drawn to go there," he notes. "But the only message I got was 'thank you for coming, thank you for trusting us.' Then the rain picked up and we got drenched — but we were laughing! It was like a cleansing."

Soon thereafter, Calgary-based angel reader Allyson Giles told Gutierrez he was to take as many people as were willing to go to the middle of the same lake so they could have their own experiences.

"I wasn't told what was going to happen, I was just told to do it," he says.

The Emerald Lake retreat, which Gutierrez has called "Dialogs of the Heart," is part of an emerging worldwide trend towards spiritual tourism, a focus on travel that brings spiritual seekers together in corners of the world reputed to invite meditation and a special connection to God.

According to the World Religious Travel Association, approximately 300 million people travel annually on journeys of spiritual exploration and together they spend an estimated $18 billion. Travel experiences counted in those figures include everything from trips to traditional religious sites such as The Vatican, Jerusalem and Medina, to other, less traditional pilgrimages to places like Stonehenge in England, Ayers Rock in Australia and Sedona in Arizona.

The so-called "New Age" concept of spiritual awakening is particularly attractive to people who have become disillusioned with the bureaucratic, at times dogmatic, nature of organized religion; sometimes their despair over the immoral behavior of some religious figures has driven them to search for a more authentic spirituality.

So where does Emerald Lake fit in?

Located in Yoho National Park in Canada's province of British Columbia, Emerald Lake is the largest of Yoho's 61 lakes and ponds. It's also one of the area's premier tourist attractions. Emerald Lake Lodge, a rustic hotel sited on the shores of the lake, caters to well-heeled sight-seers; it provides accommodation and a comfortable home base for hikers, canoeists and, in winter, cross-country skiers.

The beauty and peace of the area itself is legendary and the lake is bordered by Mount Burgess, site of the Burgess Shale, the world's most significant fossil find. It's also adjacent to Wapta Mountain and the mountains of the

President Range. This is the Canadian Rockies at their most majestic and the scenery is breath-taking.

A notable mountain guide by the name of Tom Wilson stumbled upon Emerald Lake accidentally in 1882 while he was chasing a string of errant horses and he selected the name because of the remarkable colour of the water. Later studies revealed that fine particles of glacial sediment suspended in the water are what give the lake its unusual hue. While people have known for years that the fresh mountain air and peaceful beauty of the area are conducive to relaxation, Emerald Lake has a reputation in more esoteric circles for being the home of a particularly powerful vortex of energy known as the Michael Vortex.

According to New Age philosophy, there are numerous places on Earth where special energies called vortices are thought to facilitate prayer, healing, meditation and a connection to God. Similar energy centers have been identified in places such as Stonehenge in England, Machu Picchu in Peru, and in and around the Great Pyramids of Egypt. According to New Age theory, grid lines around the Earth link these ancient sites with sources of energy deep inside the planet to create a heightened energy field. The result for people who experience this energy is said to range from feelings of exhilaration to intense self-reflection.

But enlightenment is not just a passive project; some spiritual leaders, such as Gutierrez, encourage their students to actively examine their beliefs and their behavior to find out how they've been stopping themselves from creating a more rewarding and abundant life. A week prior to the Emerald Lake trip, Gutierrez emailed each participant asking them to determine what they were seeking, what they needed to let go of, and what they would like to learn while in Emerald Lake.

While such questions might raise eyebrows in some quarters, the participants in the three-day "Dialogs of the Heart" retreat embraced the concept. All of us were already engaged in our own personal and spiritual development work; many of our number are employed or self-employed in a variety of wellness fields — health and nutritional coaching, chiropractics, or personal development. We had a grief therapist among us, a transformational radio host, several writers and a photographer.

Julie Sullivan, a real estate investor from Annapolis, Maryland, found that the retreat came at a key time in her life.

"I was going through a difficult time with my family when Daniel announced the trip," she notes. "I felt very alone and unsupported except when I was on Daniel's 40-Day calls with my spiritual friends. I decided to go on the Emerald Lake excursion to get away from my troubles, relax and spend time with my friends."

"Originally I studied the Bible and taught Christian education classes," she adds. "Pretty soon, I began to have more questions than answers, so I went outside the church and began to seek in earnest."

The path to the mid-lake meditation began on the first full day of the three-day retreat with plenty of animated conversation and an excellent and extensive breakfast served up in the Emerald Lake Lodge dining room.

Food at the Lodge is first class and the service is excellent; the lodge itself is comfortable and welcoming. The main building is made of hand-hewn timber and it features two massive stone fireplaces, several reading and sitting rooms, upper and lower verandahs, an oak bar that was salvaged from an 1890s-era Yukon saloon and comfortable conference facilities. A total of 24 cabins arranged along the shore of Emerald Lake provide accommodation for up to 200 guests. Each unit has its own fireplace, sitting room and verandah, and the site offers a modest recreation center with a fitness center, a sauna and a hot tub. A canoe rental center is located beside the gift shop.

The class convened every day in the Lodge's upstairs meeting room, although ample use was made of Nature's classroom outdoors as well.

Gutierrez comes across as an unusual spiritual leader for many reasons, not least of which is his finely-tuned sense of humor. He wears a crystal around his neck that is said to resonate with the energy of Archangel Metatron and he speaks confidently on all topics he covers with a loud and cheerful Texas accent. His shirts are well-made and outlandish, featuring a variety of bold colours and bright patterns. His laugh could stop a bull in full rampage. From time to time Gutierrez spritzes the large, open conference room with the scent of lavender and lemon grass, and although he was at one point in his life an ordained Baptist minister, his presentations to the class are accompanied by no religious fanfare.

There is, however, an obvious devotion to God in Gutierrez's work. He has a clear dedication to helping students connect with who they are at their very best moments, and to help them bring that best to bear on every aspect of their life.

"My partner and I have been coaching with Daniel for a couple of years now," says Shenna Shotwell, an entrepreneur and artist from Creedmoor, North Carolina. "We know how much our lives have changed working with him, so when he said he was having an event (in Emerald Lake), we jumped at it."

Shotwell says that she doesn't consider herself to be an especially "spiritual" person but she feels that what Gutierrez teaches represents the authentic "Good News" she's been hearing about all her life.

"I had no belief in the traditional teachings," she says. "I could not believe in some God who punishes human beings for being human beings!"

"(In Emerald Lake) it was easier for me to feel close to our Creator and *know* that there is something much larger than me at work here. Daniel has helped me to see that I *am* a child of the Universe and that I am worthy of the Blessings I receive every day."

Gutierrez is respectful of the different attitudes towards spirituality and religion among his students and his words to the class from the outset have the ring of humility.

"This is all about the experience," he begins on the first class of the weekend. "I'm very aware of the imperfection of spirituality and I think the more people are aware of the imperfection of spirituality, the better.

"(But) we're all here seeking something – the goal is to find out what that is. You called me to be here and I called you, and we want to answer the question of 'How do we become so authentic in ourselves that our authenticity transcends our world, our relationships, our businesses, in fact our authenticity transcends even our pain?'"

Gutierrez notes that what students get out of this weekend retreat will be related to how much they are willing to invest of themselves. His telephone classes follow the work of John Randolph Price, an internationally-known lecturer and author whose Abundance Book provides a guideline for 40 days of prosperity-related affirmations and meditations. Each affirmation relates to a philosophy that puts God/Source/Universe or Creator at the center of all abundance and confirms man's goodness in the eyes of that all-powerful entity.

Gutierrez has referenced the 40-Day philosophy in this retreat but has built the course primarily around his own teaching philosophy about the "Seven R's of Success."

There are unlimited training opportunities available in this world and many of them focus on prosperity, success, personal development and getting ahead. I've been to training courses that are slick and well-organized, as well as courses that are plodding and dull.

But the Gutierrez project was at once both a fruitful journey to the heart of me and a whole lot of fun. Participants were consistently friendly, upbeat and supportive of each other.

"I lift up my mind and heart to be aware, to understand, and to know that the Divine Presence of Spirit is the Source and Substance of all my good," Gutierrez recites from the Abundance program. And then we're off on an action-packed buffet of self-examination, mutual support and preparation for the journey home.

We answer questions:

"If you had no rules and this was a perfect world, what would you do?"

I answer that I would travel the world writing from my own perspective. I'm a business writer focused on corporate communications and marketing copy in my day job and I love what I do. But after decades of dedication to my trade, I've now published my first novel and am exploring other ways of using language to make a difference in the world. There's always a new horizon for me and the discovery of what that might look like is fascinating.

We play with angels:

At both the beginning and end of the retreat, Gutierrez passes around a pack of Archangel Michael meditation cards and each participant is requested to draw a card and sit meditatively with it for a few minutes. My first card says "Positive Thoughts Create Positive Results," a good choice for me since I have a history of worrying about everything that could possibly go wrong in my world. Thinking positively has sometimes required an inordinate amount of focused attention: it does not come naturally to me, although I have often wished it did.

My second card, which I draw prior to leaving the Lodge for the long trip home, says "Let go of Fear Now." I like that one, too, as it's a nice reminder that fear is, as Gutierrez and others have said, "False Evidence Appearing Real."

One of our participants is a woman by the name of Christine Riedel. She is a respected angel and animal communicator, and a Shaman, from the Toronto, Ontario, area. She teaches courses in spiritual communication and she provides consulting services to people and animals wishing to activate healing within themselves and their environment, and with others. Gutierrez invites her to deliver daily messages from the mountains, trees and lake, and she leads part of Day Two's program. The messages she delivers invite us all to be prepared to open and expand in the presence of Nature.

It's a statement about the company we're keeping that none of us seems to think this is odd. In some circles — probably most — the idea that rocks can talk is enough to cue the music for the Loony Patrol. But in this setting, with this group, there is an abiding reverence for God, humanity and every creature and entity with whom we have the honor of sharing the planet. Judgment is held to a minimum and everyone is safe to say the things they believe in their own hearts to be true.

I like that idea. Although I have never, to my knowledge, conversed with a four-legged friend, I have often thought it would be wonderful to do that.

Riedel has a thriving practice back home, which speaks to the fact that this type of thinking resonates in the hearts and minds of more people now than ever.

"It's important to remember that spirituality can be fun," she says. "We are constantly and consistently being lovingly facilitated and supported by Spirit. And it's so amazing to be able to share (that) with others.

"What's wonderful, too, is that a group of people can come together in close contact with one another and in being completely who they (are), and in honouring each other, they can truly experience Heaven on Earth."

The first day of the retreat focuses on Gutierrez's first three "R's," which he says represent the stage of an individual's decline into self-sabotage. The other four "R's," which together form what he calls "The New Perspective," focus on how to build success in our lives based on a spiritual model of the world.

Gutierrez notes that the pathway to spiritually-based abundance starts with the all-important first step of recognizing when we are resisting

"If you're not getting results, you have resistance, "he says. "The ego creates resistance because it's trying to protect you. Not being in resistance is the key."

If we don't deal with the resistance, Gutierrez notes that we slide into Resentment and then finally into Revenge. The group took part in numerous exercises to practice identifying and eliminating these first Three R's. We meditated, forgave ourselves and other significant people in our lives and listened meditatively to music. After an exhausting morning we broke for a superb lunch in the Lodge dining room.

After that it was off to the canoes. We organized ourselves into groups, found paddles and PFDs and headed out with our canoe buddies for the journey to the center of the lake. The purpose of the canoe trip was to identify what we were meant to take away from the Emerald Lake experience.

Once we were centered in the approximate middle of the lake, Gutierrez led us in a laughter meditation, which involved one minute of purposeful and enthusiastic laughter followed by sudden and complete silence. Then we settled into the fascinating project of listening for our messages.

It's a curious thing to be sitting in the middle of a lake listening for messages you are not entirely certain are going to appear. Although I am a big fan of meditation (it keeps my blood pressure down) I am no shaman, and the number of past life memories I can pull to mind is awfully limited. There is the issue of my ADD personality to factor in to the mix as well, and I was initially concerned I was going to remain parked in the starting blocks of what I feared might be the 2012 version of the Enlightenment Olympics.

But as the silence grew on me, and I realized I was easily able to keep my eyes closed with no peeking whatsoever, I began to relax. I began to feel a gradual warmth bloom throughout my body and I decided to simply stop worrying about messages and where they were coming from and just listen to the stillness, enjoy it, and even honor it. Silence is rare in my world.

Eventually a thought came from somewhere – goodness knows where — and words formed around it to tell me this retreat marked a beginning and an ending for me. It was not a complicated thought like "generosity breeds insight" or "claim your space with safety" might have been. Nor was it light-hearted such as "Kitties are sweet" or "Smile and be happy. But it was nice and it made sense and it gave me something to ponder.

Why wouldn't this be the end of one part of my life and the beginning of another?

The nuggets of wisdom other participants received ranged from "spend more time in nature with my husband" to "sing." And truly everything in between.

These messages were significant for each. As Gutierrez had already noted, we are all seeking something, and when that "something" can be distilled down into a few words of simplicity, we are so much better able to process and act upon them.

We obviously didn't need to pay good money to get to these realizations and they weren't necessarily derived from Vortex Energy. But the experience of getting to that particular emotional "lift off" point provided significant zest none of has had previously accessed.

Beth McBlain is a PR consultant from Toronto, Canada, and she found the overall matrix of the Emerald Lake retreat gave her a sense of new beginnings as well.

"I felt that it was a take-off point for me on my spiritual journey," she notes. "I don't have a lot of spiritual friends and it was nice to have a community where I could be open and speak directly from my heart about what I really feel.

"My spirituality is not something I've shared with very many people," McBlain adds. "(But) there were like-minded people and souls (at Emerald Lake) and I realized I wasn't an alien. It felt really good to be part of a community."

After the canoe meditation, the group rounded out the day with some free time, a nice dinner, and a two-hour hike around the lake before dark. These are the diamond times of a personal retreat, where we each make tentative efforts to expand into each other's worlds, to get to know how our companions see and experience the world around them. I was struck by how humble everyone was, despite the many accomplishments collected over decades of experience. And I realized quite fully how not everyone would find a spiritual retreat an agreeable way to vacation. This is about going deep down inside and looking at what is there. And also, perhaps, what is missing.

One of the many fun highlights of this particular retreat was the competition for Oscar, the replica Academy Award statue Gutierrez had brought along with him from LA.

He believes that when we are not achieving at our desired level of accomplishment, many of us break out our "stories" — e.g. "I wasn't able to succeed because my mother, father, brother, sister, or uncle was mean, abusive, angry, absent, distant, selfish or whatever."

As we shared our thoughts over the weekend, many of us slipped into the drama of our pasts and got lost in the mystery of our own misfortunes. Whenever this happened, Gutierrez would cheerfully take the Oscar and place it in front of the "story teller" as a not-so-subtle reminder to stop making excuses. Although Oscar changed hands many times, he ultimately went home with Tony Edgell, a good-natured and extremely perceptive life coach from Lancashire, Pennsylvania.

"Results are sometimes harsh, always fair," Gutierrez noted. "You are the common denominator of your own experiences."

The last half of the Emerald Lake Retreat focused on what Gutierrez called the New Perspective: Releasing, Receiving, Rejoicing and Re-engaging.

Releasing was about getting rid of trapped emotion or old, outdated paradigms;

Receiving was about learning to graciously receive the abundance of the Universe;

Rejoicing was about the importance of gratitude and the value of joyfully celebrating successes as they occur and

Re-engaging was about how to return to our work-a-day lives and be more vibrantly true to ourselves wherever we go.

"Utopia exists inward," Gutierrez says. "And you want to be vulnerable enough to be you, but strong enough that you don't give yourself away."

Gutierrez noted that re-engagement is about taking the risk to be more of ourselves, trusting our intuition and saying "yes" to opportunities more often. He cautioned that this didn't mean saying "yes" indiscriminately, because, as he pointed out, "When I say no to others, I'm also saying yes to myself."

The afternoon of Day Two of the retreat involved a hike up the mountain at the far end of Emerald Lake with veteran Canadian hiker Dave Albano. His mission is to climb every mountain in the Canadian Rockies and he was pleased to share his love of the mountains with our group.

"This is just a sliver of what my life has become," he noted. "Yoho is a Cree word for 'a place of awe and wonder.' That's what this place is, in the literal sense of the word. I like to think big and I like to act big, and when I get to the top of a mountain, I get to touch the face of God."

We said our good-byes at the end of the retreat feeling the warmth of new friendships and the strength of new insights. I personally felt peaceful and restored. I didn't know how I was going to be moving forward through my life or what was going to change for me, but I was certain that there would be some changes. Aside from deepening my connection to a lot of superb people, I felt a lot had shifted inside me, much of it represented in an interesting experience I had during one of our meditation breaks.

Gutierrez had played the song "Coming Home," by Gwyneth Paltrow, and then dismissed the class into half an hour of silence. The instruction to stay silent for half an hour was a challenge for me. I enjoy conversation very much but I took the directions to heart and picked my way down the overgrown embankment in front of the lodge to get to the lakeshore. There were trees and shrubs, sticks, brambles and weeds blocking my way and although I searched for an easy path down, I couldn't find one.

By the time I got to the waterfront I was scratched and a little frustrated. I found a large flat rock on which to sit and I drank in the magnificence of my view. The lake was calm, the trees were whispering in the wind, and the massive mountains presided over the world around me. Birds sang and swallows swooped and danced low over the water as I sat. I thought about the clarity of the water here. How grateful I was for friends and family. How perfect life is in its imperfections. How safe I felt.

At the end of the half-hour I stood and turned, bracing myself for the effort of clawing my way back through the bushes and brambles to the top of the hill, but content with the idea even so. I was stunned, however, to see, before my very eyes, a straight path going right up to the top of the hill towards the lodge again. No brambles. No bushes. Just a clear straight path leading directly to where I wanted to go.

I could have sworn the path hadn't been there before. Or had I just not had the eyes with which to see it? I'm still puzzled about that one. Is Reality really that flexible?

This seems to be the message Gutierrez wants to impart. Whatever we desire is at the fingertips of our awareness but we need to expand our scope of vision in order to actually see it all.

That expansion idea appeals to me. The vision part, too. And if everything I want is already mine, then I guess it's up to me to embrace it cheerfully and enjoy it whole-heartedly. My spirit soars at the very idea. What an amazing vacation.

40 Days of Spiritual Follow-Up:

The Emerald Lake "Dialogs of the Heart" retreat was a full experience where friendships were formed and deepened, insights were gained, and old, limiting beliefs transmuted into new supportive ones. But the journey continued for 10 participants for another 40 days after the trip ended as they took part in a "40 Days of Integration" follow-up telephone coaching program with tour leader Daniel Gutierrez.

The call followed the spiritual affirmations set out in John Randolph Price's "Abundance Book," but participants were also required to each set both a professional goal and a personal goal. The plan was to apply the learning of the "7 R's" program covered in Emerald Lake and, in the context of a group coaching experience, work towards the fulfillment of everyone's goals.

Gutierrez required that the goals represent massive accomplishments for each participant.

For an hour a day these students supported each other with Gutierrez's guidance, and shared their experiences through a special private Facebook page. The experience was demanding and intense, and one participant chose to drop out.

At the end of 40 days, however, the nine remaining members of the group had created $80,000 in income, written three books, completed one award-winning work of art and accomplished two feats of derring-do (one individual went sky-diving and another tackled rock climbing). Weight was lost, beauty was rediscovered, fitness was regained and social lives were renewed.

The scope of accomplishment was sweeping and humbling and required enormous amounts of focus and effort. But in the end, it all proved the point Gutierrez often makes in his coaching with clients: Successful people do what unsuccessful people don't do.

Beth McBlain, a Public Relations consultant from Toronto, Canada, summed the process up succinctly:

"So many people believe that being spiritual means you have to give up the luxuries of life but that's not Daniel's message. You don't need to be on the ground in a tent in the rain to be spiritual — you can stay at a five-star hotel and be comfortable.

"And you *can* have it all."

Haven't Had Enough of You

A True Story

When my oldest daughter was a toddler she would resist going to bed with might and main, and when I finally tucked her in well past her bedtime she would collapse into a marathon of tragic tears.

"But I haven't had enough of you," she would sob.

It broke my heart to see her so sad. I was a self-employed single mom at the time and I was exhausted.

"You'll see more of me tomorrow," I'd soothe. "It'll be okay. You'll see." Despite my calm words I hadn't had enough of her, either, but I needed to roam alone around our little home and absorb the solace of a quiet house.

"But I want more of you NOW," she would protest.

As the years rolled on, we both became swept up in the rhythm of life. My daughter started school and I fell in love. She started piano lessons and I re-married. She got braces; I made more babies.

One day I woke up and realized, with a shock, that the little girl I had cosseted and cared for was leaving the next day to start university in a distant town. How was it possible that this beautiful child I had borne a heartbeat ago had grown up so quickly? How had those precious years spun themselves into the fragile silk of memory? I was melancholic and morose that day. As the evening sped into night I felt abandoned and bereft. My baby was leaving me.

That night, after she retired to her room, I stared sadly at the ceiling and thought of all the little adventures we had shared together, all the adventures that were no longer possibilities. I climbed the stairs and knocked on her bedroom door.

"Come in," she said. I opened the door and peeked in. Her suitcases were packed and sitting at the end of her bed, and her reading lamp cast a gentle glow on her youthful, hopeful face.

I burst into tears.

"MOM!" she gasped. "What's wrong?"

I crossed the room and crawled into bed beside her.

"I haven't had enough of you," I sobbed.

She hugged me fiercely and started to cry too.

"It'll be okay," she soothed through tears. "You'll see."

I didn't see. But she had things to do that didn't involve me. And she needed a little time to roam around the world and absorb the adventure of a waiting universe. I had been adventurous too, once, and I had travelled my world meeting new people and trying new things. How do we lose our taste for the unexpected in life, that we stop daring, dreaming, and driving ourselves onto a new horizon? How had I become so locked into a life of staid regularity?

The next morning, she left to home to study hard and make me proud. After four years of Canadian education, years in which my husband died and my other children grew, my daughter announced that she was moving to England to pursue a master's degree in journalism.

"But, that's SO FAR AWAY!" I moaned.

"It'll be okay, Mom," she said. I wasn't so sure.

I had embarked upon an education of my own, one that required me to re-invent myself as the widowed mother of two young children. It was lonely and difficult, and the transition required me to redefine my life in the light of my own hopes and dreams. Did I even have any of those anymore? Was anything ever going to be okay again?

My daughter carried on, finished her education and landed a wonderful job in England. She was, and still is, happy, and I've been glad that she has found her wings.

Somewhere along the way it occurred to me that I still might have wings of my own, too. It occurred to me that maybe I could find them again, try them on, test them out. My daughter has blazed a trail of adventure and certainty for herself, a trail I had travelled myself so many years ago. Maybe that trail was still out there for me, somewhere, waiting for me to step back aboard.

The other day I Skyped my big little girl in great excitement: "I'm going trekking in Nepal in September!" I announced. It was something I had always wanted to do and a plan had fallen together for me out of the blue.

"You're WHAT?!" she gasped.

"Nepal," I said, helpfully.

"Nepal," she said flatly.

"Yes, Nepal," I said firmly. It occurred to me that she might think mothers shouldn't go trekking in Nepal.

"M-o-o-o-m?" she asked finally, gently even.

I braced myself: "Yes Sweetie

"Can I come with you?"

I gasped in delight.

Years ago, I never could have imagined a shared adventure with my daughter and all the sadness that had crystallized in tears wrought by the pain of separation dissolved in that one perfect moment.

It was all so daring and perfect, and it made me realize yet again how powerful the circle of life really is – nothing but beginnings, endings and transitions to another fresh start. I'm deliriously eager, now, for whatever shows up next in my bumpy discovery of the life I'm leading; the adventure is magical.

We haven't had enough indeed.

Getting Away, Gaining Insight

A Writer in Nepal

A True Story

I could never have imagined the depth of experience two weeks in Nepal would deliver and I have no doubt that the sights, sounds, smells and memories of Kathmandu and points beyond will stay with me for a very long time.

The travels my daughter and I experienced within this small country perched between China and India will no doubt enlighten my writing in surprising ways, and I can't wait to see what bubbles up over the next few years.

But describing what I did and saw will be easier than trying to encapsulate the emotional experience of being in a Third World country for the first time. I've come home with a renewed sense of how privileged I am to live in a place where electricity, hot water and medical care are always at my fingertips.

The 36 hours it took to get to Nepal were like a passage to another time, another world. This is a country where cows roam the streets at will and killing one, even accidentally, is punishable by 20 years in jail. There is a large wild dog population in Nepal and they all seemed to spend their days sleeping comfortably on sidewalks or beside public monuments. I could hear them howling and barking at night as they did whatever wild dogs do in the dark.

Sometimes I wasn't sure the barking I heard was canine in origin. Sometimes it was a chilling sound.

We saw a variety of other types of wildlife in urban settings in Nepal as well – chickens, goats and monkeys seemed to be everywhere and how they all maintained their lives in the relentless stream of traffic was beyond me.

In Kathmandu, at least, the streets were filled with all manner of vehicles, and drivers seemed to have an intuitive sense of space and a kind of impeccable timing that I don't think I could replicate.

We visited many historic sites in Nepal, and some were UNESCO world heritage sites, ancient and steeped in mystery. We also saw the country's living Goddess, the Kumari, a young girl whose glance is rare and highly prized.

Heading into the mountains we were part of a ceremony dedicated to the consecration of land on an organic coffee plantation and we were both blessed by the Hindu priest who performed the ceremony. Buddhist monks at a mountain top monastery said prayers for me, my daughter and our travelling companions, and the hand-made metal singing bowl I purchased at a traditional bowl maker's shop was blessed by the abbot of another Buddhist monastery.

At a book signing in a classical and very beautiful garden, my daughter and I met Shyalpa Tenzin Rinpoche, author of "Living Fully," a book about finding calm and purpose in a modern world.

We took a small airplane ride along the spine of the Himalayas and saw Mount Everest from the air. We spoke with a miller's daughter in a rural village. We witnessed a traditional witch doctor performing channelled healing rituals on people suffering a variety of ailments and I climbed to the sacred Temple of Wishes where people brought goats, chickens and pigeons to be sacrificed in the pursuit of their heart-felt hopes for their lives and those they loved.

In short, the kaleidoscope of life that swept past our eyes and hearts in Nepal was dizzying and vast. We're home now and carried away again by the hectic rhythm of work and family, business and life.

The time with the girl who made me a mother was magical and full of explorations and conspiracies. It was a time of vast observation and reflection. I'm back at my keyboard and whirling through deadlines and plans for the future. Life is busy and full.

But part of me is still gazing out over the mountainsides and terraced rice fields of what is undoubtedly one of the most beautiful countries on Earth. I look at my daughter and we laugh together at the exhilaration of being in Nepal — Nepal! We are on a joint adventure, it seems, even while apart.

The words will come.

Good writing meets French countryside

New thoughts on old ideas
A True Story

The corn has barely started pushing up through loamy fields of black soil but the trees are in full leaf and the dry roads curving through the village of Saint-Coutant in central France no doubt still echo with the joy of the traditional French wedding I attended last weekend in this beautiful corner of the world.

Hidden huntsmen discharge their rifles into the scorching summer sky as invited guests follow a marching band from the bride and groom's home to the village Mayor's office. The bride cuts ribbons stretched across the road and lights colourful "fires of joy" that friends and neighbours set on the road for the occasion. It's a cheerful affair, full of laughter, dancing and bubbling conversation.

The day is full of contrasts and I'm struck by the beautiful way opposites combine to create new meaning. The wedding follows a formula handed down by generations of French farm folk, for example, but the bride and groom are veterans of divorce wars and have been living happily together for many years.

What strikes me most of all, however, is the fact that while this wonderful wedding unfolds completely in French, the bride and groom, their families and many of their friends, are primarily English-speaking expats from the UK, many of whom have thrown themselves into communicating in French – and improving their skill with the language — whenever possible.

The harmony is impressive.

At the wedding reception I attended, rivers of English and French conversation sped along throughout the day and long into the night accompanied by quiet streams of Italian, German and Dutch, gentle reminders of an even larger world. Precision was not required, nor was it expected, and everyone overlooked linguistic errors in the great adventure of understanding.

I'm struck by how this "laissez-passer" approach to communication is impossible with written language.

When we try to speak a language that is not entirely our own, we can continually refine what we mean with a word, a glance, an upraised eyebrow or a helpless shrug of the shoulders. It's a kind of verbal and physical editing process that eventually results in understanding.

When we write, by contrast, we plant the words on a page and hope our meaning is clear – the printed words remain static in a kind of unyielding testimony to our ability to communicate.

I once heard it said that we rarely sound as intelligent in another language as we do in our own and I would add that I think we can also seem far less clever and insightful when we write in our own language.

There is a craft involved in writing that is mercifully absent when we speak, and I've met many highly talented and creative people who appear somewhat less so on paper or online because their skill with words hasn't kept pace with their surging abilities in other areas.

And perhaps that's why freelance writers like me stay in business — skill with the written word is still valued, still necessary, and still a wonderful way to light the delightful "fires of joy" that help warm readers' hearts.

Words at Play: English Musings

A True Story

The climb up the side of the hill in West Sussex was bathed in conversation, sunshine and all the delight of rediscovering a favoured corner of a world, I feared I'd left behind forever, years ago.

Gentle spring breezes played with hope and two of my children ran ahead on the footpath to scamper over stiles, chase stray cats and examine tracks in the mud that might have been made by a fox.

Birds twittered, crocuses bloomed and at my side the girl who turned me into a mother chatted with the girl who knew me way back when I thought I might want to be a writer someday. She is one of my oldest and best friends.

The years touched us kindly in England last spring.

Along the top of the South Downs in England runs a track that legend says was made before there was an England, before the language we now speak had yet been uttered. It extends for miles, threading its way from Winchester in the west to the village of Alfriston in the east.

The track has retained a gracefully rugged complexion for centuries and from along its winding spine unfolds the breathtaking English countryside to one side and the majestic unease of the English Channel some miles off on the other.

The view is startlingly beautiful but more breathtaking still is the perspective a trek along the South Downs can deliver: on one side is the life we brought with us on the journey, along the top is the unexpected exploration of ideas we might like to pursue, and away in the direction we have not yet travelled is a world of possibility, a path not yet sharply focused.

It is a reminder to breathe.

Life can be a turbulent journey at times and the energy that ignites the first few decades does not always burn consistently thereafter; there on the crest of southern England, however, with children's laughter ringing in my ears years and an old friend's conversation keeping me grounded in good English soil, I felt energized and renewed.

The vacation is over now but the benefits linger and while the maple leaf is decidedly forever, I have to admit that over an important part of my heart, for some romantic reason, Britannia still rules.

I Love the Library. Again

A True Story

I am ashamed to say it but my last trip to a public library occurred almost a decade ago and it ended in tears as my two youngest children, both toddlers, ran through the stacks pulling random books off shelves and laughing loudly as I raced behind them trying to regain control. This was not my finest moment and the trauma ever after lay not so much in the memory of their misbehaviour as in the realization that my children might never sit still long enough to learn to read.

The months rolled on and life was busy. With the Internet fulfilling my every research need, the library became a background memory that no longer held great relevance.

When a recent business meeting took me to my local public library's main branch, however, I was astounded at the explosion in resources that's taken place over the past ten years. It's not just about friendly books and loaner CDs anymore! The online accessibility of resources surprised me the most: anyone with a library card can access thousands of online databases – reliable ones — on any topic you can imagine and help is available with any research users undertake. The library in my home town also offers:

• downloadable eBooks and audio books
• free DVD loans

- free wireless internet
- pre-packaged book selections to grab 'n go
- help with web research for genealogical projects
- an interactive career search reference resource
- FWii Wii for big screen Wii game enjoyment
- a dial-a-story service for children
- resources in numerous languages
- literacy tutoring
- many services for visually and audially impaired people

And so much more! The library offers a wide range of resources for children and teens and online reference help is available via email or instant messaging. In essence, the library has changed from a temple to the written word to a repository of practical resources applicable to almost any aspect of today's world. If there is any information I need about almost anything, I know I can probably get it through my library.

How did this happen?

I suspect that "response to consumer demand" has a lot to do with it and I applaud the Library for doing a terrific job of staying current: it's an exciting place to go! Even my children – who somehow turned into voracious readers with many interests – are happy in a library now and as a family we're looking at the library as a destination again, if only, sometimes, on a virtual plane.

Those dark distant days of Library Rumble are long behind us now and easier days lie ahead. Thank goodness!

The Fictional Stories

A Change of Plan

A Short Story

The elevator doors closed and Tara Sloane took a deep breath as she began the slow descent to the ground floor of the luxurious office tower in which she worked.

She checked her appearance in the mirror and smiled grimly. It had been the worst meeting of her whole life and despite an absolutely perfect haircut, she was feeling queasy. Should she go along with Brock McCallion's request to help with what was clearly an illegal act? Or should she call the police? The money he offered in exchange for her help was awfully tempting.

Tara tapped a beautifully lacquered fingernail on the soft pale skin of her chin as she considered her choices. What to do, what to do?

She'd been working at Dade-Jansen Securities for only three years but in that time she had become indispensible to the team at the heart of Canada's largest investment firm. Initially hired as an administrative assistant, Tara was now responsible for coordinating the firm's bank liaison program and she alone verified all trading transactions.

Tara's pay had risen in keeping with her growing responsibilities and although she was earning more than she had ever thought possible, she still couldn't keep up with the expenses involved in dating Derek Marquesson. Derek was seven years older than Tara, and he was just her kind of guy. He earned a fortune as a successful bond trader in a competing firm and he was a man who knew how to enjoy life. His father owned a large transportation company and the family lived well on every continent.

In fact, Tara had met Derek the previous year at her cousin's wedding in Ibiza and the two had hit it off immediately. The wedding celebrations had continued joyfully well into the night and when the sun had risen over the horizon the next morning, it had found Tara and Derek locked in intimate embrace. Given that they both lived and worked in Toronto, it was only natural that they would see each other upon their return. They had been pursuing an enormously enjoyable relationship ever since, although Derek's job meant he was not available around the clock. Tara was quite certain they were in love.

Tara's parents were financially comfortable and she had grown up in a large stone house in a tony Toronto neighbourhood. She had attended all the schools a well-bred young lady ought to attend.

But when she reached age 25 her monthly allowance from her parents was reduced to a fraction of what it once had been and her parents told her that the family fortune would no longer be available to bail her out every time her spending exploded beyond her income. She had to learn how to manage her money more prudently, they said, and they warned that she was headed for trouble if she didn't sharpen up.

Tara didn't think her parents needed to be so mean. Truth to tell, their selfishness had been terribly hurtful. They had plenty of money. Why wouldn't they share it with her? She was never going to manage on the paltry sum Dade-Janssen gave her if her parents refused to support her financially. In fact, she had been on the verge of starting the tedious process of wheedling an increase out of her father when he had cut her back. Now what? Self-sufficiency was impossible!

Although Tara had no clue how she might go about completing this independence project on her own, it struck her that marriage might be a viable option and she had just decided that it was an idea worth pursuing when Derek tangoed into her life.

Their Toronto romance had been delightful so far. Although Derek paid the freight for most of the young couple's entertainment, there was a lot of pressure on Tara to dress the part of the sophisticated girlfriend and enjoy those little luxuries that would show Derek how much alike they were. She had to pony up for five hundred dollar shoes and thousand dollar dresses.

There had also been lingering Sunday lunches at trendy – and very pricey – downtown restaurants, beautiful new designer light fixtures for her sweet little condo, and regular rounds of micro-dermabrasion facials with IPL light therapy to keep her skin aglow with the beauty of youth.

It was all crushing her financially but when Derek finally married her – hopefully soon – she'd be set for life.

Great guy, great holidays, expensive cars and dinners out every night of the week. Derek would make sure she was flush with cash. Forever.

The problem was that until that all came to pass, Tara had to make ends meet on her own. She had run up a mass of debt on her credit cards and she could find no reasonable way to pay it all off. If she didn't do something – and soon – she would prove that her parents had been right after all and her pride would never survive the humiliation. She just needed to keep everything together long enough to get the ring on her finger. When that happened she would somehow manage to swing a debit card that led directly to Derek's bank account and a credit card that practically begged to be used. When was he ever going to pop the question?

Meanwhile, Brock McCallion and his colleagues had been running up a little debt of their own and it was keeping them awake at night. The firm had been losing massive amounts of money on clients' trading accounts for the past year and Brock was worried. No, Brock was way past worried – he was stressing every moment of every day about how to get himself out of this mess with his reputation intact. He and the firm's accountant, Chet Barker, had been as creative as they possibly could be with the firm's accounting and so far they'd been able to keep the news about the firm's appalling performance secret. The wealthy clients who had been paying for the firm's annual general meetings in exotic locations were none the wiser.

But the game was almost up.

Losses were growing. The auditors were bound to figure out what had been happening at the year-end Moment of Truth but Brock and Chet were hoping to solve the problem before that came to pass. If some files disappeared and the company's computer system was disabled by a treacherous virus, and maybe all of the firm's backup files were accidentally damaged or deleted as well, then maybe they could end-run reality. They had everything planned down to the smallest detail. They just needed someone to push a few buttons.

Tara was not a computer genius but she did have plenty of training in how to manipulate the Dade-Janssen computer system. She had attended countless hours of annoying courses in the subject and she was actually quite proud to realize that she knew the firm's computer system almost as well as she knew the Harrod's online catalogue. Not that it did her any good, she thought tartly.

Brock had offered her a tantalizing deal: if she would simply orchestrate a complete computer meltdown they would double her salary and provide a one-time cash payment large enough to pay all her debts and leave a little extra cash sitting around for something fun. She knew full well the move was illegal. But as Brock had explained to her, "No one would ever know." Brock was a smart guy – he knew about these things.

Didn't he?

Tara was going to think about it over night and give Brock her answer in the morning. She was in a tight spot, to say the least. She was an honest girl, more or less, and she didn't want to get into trouble with the Law. Her parents would have a fit. *If* anyone ever found out about it.

On the other hand, Derek had invited her to a week-long party at a friend's house in Gibraltar week after next. She needed an entire new wardrobe and an overseas airfare. She needed spending money and party money. If she didn't keep up with Brock and go wherever he went, there was always the chance he would meet another pretty blonde girl to play with. No! This man was *hers*! She needed him.

By the time the elevator doors opened at the ground level of the 70-storey building in the downtown core, Tara had made up her mind.

After enduring a restless sleep, she returned to work the next morning and spoke briefly with Brock McCallion. She called Derek and left a message on his voicemail. Maybe tonight if he was available she would take him to that cute little French bistro that had opened recently on Queen Street – just to show him how much she loved him. The way to a man's heart…

At 10:40 she typed the correct coding into her computer. It was surprisingly difficult to hit the "Enter" key and after about 15 agonizing minutes of hesitation, she deleted the coding and stood up. She was committed to the idea but she needed a little liquid courage first. A drink to calm her nerves. And what if somebody *did* find out?

The bar at the restaurant downstairs opened at 11:00 and Tara shook with apprehension as she texted Derek again. Maybe he would like to meet her for lunch, too? It wasn't like him to take so long to answer her calls. He must be in a meeting. The delight she should have been feeling at the guarantee of prolonging her affair long enough to bring it to its logical and happy conclusion still had not appeared. Tara's feet felt like lead as she walked to the bathroom and vomited in the third stall. This had been happening a lot lately and she wondered if she had picked up a virus.

She didn't feel like eating but she was sure she would feel better if she put something in her stomach. Tara hesitated a moment before entering the expensive steak house located on the ground floor of her office building.

The smell of fried onions and grilled meat was overpowering but she squared her shoulders and walked in regardless. The shrimp salad in this restaurant was divine.

Tara ordered a glass of champagne to celebrate her bravado and she stared glumly at the bubbles making their steady way up to the surface of the liquid as she waited for her lunch to arrive. Across the room she caught sight of Derek and she was about to rush over to throw her arms around him when she realized he was not alone. The blonde sitting practically in his lap was laughing and spooning caviar into his appreciative mouth. He stroked the hand that held the spoon and caressed the collar of the woman's light blouse ever so gently, possessively, before he sat forward to take a mouthful of Perrier.

Tara stared at them in shock. How could this possibly be?!

She slumped back in her chair in a rage. She was all set to rush over and crash that Perrier bottle right over Derek's head, and the blonde's too, just for good measure. But no, Tara prided herself on her self-control. There was a better way to handle this. But how dare he be such a spineless two-timing jerk? He had been playing with her the whole time!

The shrimp salad arrived and Tara downed the rest of her champagne before handing her empty glass to the waiter with a demand for another.

"And for pity's sake bring me your good stuff this time," she snapped as he bowed courteously in understanding.

"OK, girl, now think, think, think," she muttered to herself. Derek and the blonde were still cooing at each other as their meals arrived – sushi for her, steak and lobster for him. He was going to get fat if he kept that up, thought Tara. She was three-quarters of the way through her shrimp salad and finally at the end of her third glass of champagne when she had a flash of brilliance. He was not going to get away with ruining her future that easily!

Tara picked up her Chanel bag and rose majestically from her seat. She walked slowly across the restaurant, the silk of her Fendi skirt swaying gently above her knees. She pasted a pert little smile on her face and stood beside Derek waiting for him to notice her. He and the blonde were deep in conversation and Tara noticed the blonde was wearing Prada. Prada? That was for *old* women!

The blonde noticed her first and Tara watched with satisfaction as an annoyed look crossed the woman's face.

"Hi Derek," Tara said cheerfully." Derek looked at her in shock. Tara pulled a chair up right beside his and sat down daintily at their table. She smiled sweetly and rested her chin on one hand.

"How's lunch?" she asked, teasingly, staring deep into his eyes. The blonde's jaw dropped almost to her knees as Tara leaned forward and kissed Derek gently on the cheek. "I know you have a thing for older women but really, Derek, don't you think you've taken it a little bit too far this time?" Tara spared a pitying look for the blonde, who now appeared to be gasping for air. Derek still hadn't found the courage to speak.

"I *am* his *wife*," the blonde spat.

Tara didn't even look at the woman and she leaned over to whisper a little sloppily in Derek's ear.

"I'll tell you what, Derek," she said. "Pay my bill for that lovely lunch I just enjoyed today and clear off all my debt along with an outrageously generous bonus for good behaviour and I won't make a loud noise about the nine-month flu you've given me. Reject my offer and I will make the scene of a century right here, right now. You have one minute."

Derek looked as though he were going to choke. But he took out his chequebook and began to write.

"What are you *doing*, Derek?" his wife hissed.

Derek, defeated, just sighed. "I'll tell you later," he said. The wife stared at Tara with venomous eyes.

Tara picked up the cheque and surveyed the amount, surprised he had been so generous. She smiled sweetly.

"Thank you Derek," she said happily. She rose and strolled out of the restaurant, her purse swinging jauntily at her side. At the elevator doors she paused. She smiled and punched three numbers into the keypad of her Smartphone.

"I'd like to report a crime," she said softly. Things were going to be different now.

Marking the Mink

A Short Story

Gabrielle pushed her cart to the frozen desserts section of her favourite grocery store and nervously surveyed the crowd gathered half way down the aisle.

She had learned of Price Chopper's special sale on Haagen Dazs Double Chocolate Swirl ice cream through a banner ad in the store's Wednesday afternoon flyer. She knew that the 50 per cent discount was only valid "while supplies last" and she cursed herself for sleeping in past the store opening that morning. What was wrong with her anyway? Why hadn't she arrived earlier? Shoppers were limited to three containers per person but Gabrielle doubted supplies would last long enough for her to proudly grab her fair share and dash out into the crisp winter morning. Couldn't she do anything right?

Double Chocolate Swirl happened to be the favourite ice cream of Gabrielle's partner, Gray, and given that she had regretfully, if accidentally, used the rear bumper of his beautiful 1968 Mustang GT convertible to make friends with a telephone pole parked mysteriously, nay, even *invisibly* – in an inconvenient location the night before, she was very anxious to make amends.

A few tubs of ice cream would obviously not repair the damage to Gray's pet vehicle, nor would it repair, to any great extent, a relationship that was now hobbling along under a cloud of anger and reproach. But it might reassure Gray that Gabrielle was at least trying to make amends, and that she was sorry for her carelessness. Maybe he would change his mind about spending another night on the couch. Maybe he wouldn't be so cold to her anymore. Maybe they could patch things up one more time. Maybe.

But would she be able to get close enough to Freezer #11 to snare her peace offering? And if she did end up within arm's reach of the chilly chocolaty treat would there even be any ice cream left to snatch? In the 18 months that she and Gray had been sharing a home, Gabrielle had learned that peace campaigns were delicate operations. It seemed she was always launching another one, and she thought she was getting quite good at them.

Step Number One was to take full and complete responsibility for her transgression. Today it was the crashing of Gray's beloved car. In recent weeks, she had also owned up to accidentally ruining his favourite shirt with bleach, carelessly ripping a hole in his favourite chair with her sewing scissors, losing his favourite hammer while she was hanging pictures for a neighbour and breaking a china plate that had been given to his parents on their wedding day. She was such a klutz and now a nervous wreck to boot. She felt like she never did anything right.

But at least she freely admitted the truth about her inadequacies. There were so many of them to embrace that she felt like all she ever did was repair the damage she'd done to her relationship with this guy. She had become the mistress of accountability and it was exhausting.

Step Number Two in the campaign to wiggle her way back into her man's good graces was to apologize. She was always truly very sorry for her screw-ups and she couldn't believe how reckless, careless or neglectful she had been. She told Gray as much, and she knew that when she looked up at him with her saddest puppy dog eyes he would thaw, just a little and lean towards forgiveness, if only for a few moments. He was a forgiving guy, really.

But it took Step Number Three to really hit a homer: she had to make it up to him. Sometimes she would make amends by preparing Gray's favourite meal or surprising him with tickets to a baseball game. He loved baseball. Sometimes she would even tuck a couple of chocolate bars into his lunch before he left for work in the morning. Chocolate was Gray's biggest weakness; Haagen Daaz Double Chocolate Swirl ice cream made him practically delirious with delight. Gabrielle needed this ice cream. She needed a win. She needed Gray.

The two had met at a mutual friend's house one searing July evening when the word "barbecue" guaranteed that complete strangers could melt together in the joy of a Canadian summer. They both liked volleyball, romantic movies and beach volleyball. They both had older brothers. And they both loved Gray's sweet little Mustang convertible. This was clearly a match made in heaven and the two had been inseparable ever since.

The only challenge to the romance was Gray's refusal to commit. After a year-and-a-half of living together he still wasn't sure about that big jump into Forever and he had been making ominous statements about needing a little more "space."

Gabrielle found this focus on space quite puzzling but she kept quiet about it. Angry accusations would only confirm his suspicion that they might not be p-e-r-f-e-c-t together. Gabrielle had learned over the course of her 26 years on the planet that getting along with people meant keeping quiet and giving in. You had to be agreeable and keep your head down. You had to suck it up and stick it out. Anger never solved anything. Especially when it came to Gray. He had enough anger for both of them.

Gabrielle had considered turning up the heat on her campaign to marry the man of her dreams by having an "accident" that might result in the "nine-month flu" — but she reasoned that the risk of him refusing responsibility for the new little life she might create was simply too high.

She had thought about popping the question herself, but then realized her pride simply could not bear the pain of a potential rejection; if Gray turned her down, she would have to move out altogether or die of shame. Gabrielle had played with the idea of developing a series of flirtations with attractive men they both knew, but she decided Gray was more likely to send her packing than propose marriage during an anguished flush of bitter jealousy.

Gabrielle had talked to Gray's mother, his brother and the lady at the dry cleaner's but none of them had any suggestions for making Gray see how badly he needed to marry her. No, it was possible that Gray was just not the marrying kind.

Unfortunately, Gabrielle *was* the marrying kind. She had wanted to get married since the day she first saw Cinderella kiss her celluloid Prince Charming wearing that gorgeous white wedding gown and huge pearl earrings. She had confirmed her desire for a wedding when Sleeping Beauty, Snow White and all those other Disney princesses stepped boldly into Gabrielle's conscious awareness and beckoned her to follow them into the state of holy matrimony. Her mother's third wedding was just the fuel her fire needed: living together was nice, her mother had said, but a wedding was forever.

Gabrielle couldn't wait to see for herself.

She'd had boyfriends in the past – well, maybe one or two – but none were as suave, gentle, fun and industrious as Gray. In addition to his beautiful fire-engine red convertible, he owned a sleek black vintage Trans-Am, a power boat with twin 80-horsepower Mercury engines and a cute little bungalow in an established part of town. He rarely complained. If he was unhappy about something, he'd argue and yell as loudly as the next guy. And then he'd move on. It was the moving on part that concerned Gabrielle right now.

Although all those klutzy things she'd been doing lately were mostly unavoidable, she wondered if a tiny little part of her was punishing Gray for not *wanting* her enough, for caring too little, for being willing to let her slip through his fingers. She wasn't sure he actually *would* let her go. So far he had stayed in the game. But was she pushing her luck?

She spent a lot of time fretting about how to make him happy. Was he happy? Was he in love? Or was she kidding herself when she thought that he would eventually come to his senses and slide a ring on her finger? He always looked as though he were afraid to breathe. What did he have to worry about? She was the one who was losing weight over the issue, and she had started spending a lot of time crying. What if she wasn't good enough for Gray? What if she wasn't good enough for anyone?

The Double Chocolate Swirl was bound to win him over, she muttered to herself. Getting it for him was clearly an act of love. Maybe he'd marry her then?

As Gabrielle stood at the edge of the crowd planning her assault on both the ice cream and her one true love, she began to feel overwhelmed by panic. She had just begun to dissolve into a paroxysm of stress over her inability to land a man when a beautifully preserved woman in black mink steamed confidently past her and headed towards the freezer.

"Confidence," thought Gabrielle "That's all it takes," and she followed the woman's lead.

The clutter of humanity at Freezer #11 was a throbbing mess of grabbing hands and hostile words. With the freezer door wedged fully opened there was limited opportunity for people to traffic their booty out to their waiting carts but that didn't slow Mink Lady down one little bit. Gabrielle edged to the outside of the crowd to wait her turn beside the woman. She might be anywhere between the ages of 42 and 75, Gabrielle surmised. Her nails were lacquered a saucy shade of red and from her ears dangled large triangular-shaped crystals that could not possibly be diamonds. Could they? Nobody with diamonds shopped at Price Chopper! Fur was unheard of in this store as well, for that matter. What was this lady doing here?

The lady turned her head to look at Gabrielle, aware of her scrutiny and not at all happy about it. She looked Gabby up and down, from the dark roots peaking through the faded blonde straw of hair at the crown of Gabrielle's head to the scuffed and frayed shoes that adorned her feet.

The lady sneered, raised an eyebrow and, in a deep, throaty voice snarled. "I was here first."

Somewhat taken aback, Gabby shuffled forward a little as the crowd moved ahead. What on Earth could she possibly say to that?

But before she could make a snappy reference to the fact that, yes, the woman had obviously arrived on the planet many years before Gabrielle had shown up, the woman turned back towards the freezer and began pushing the people in front of her aside with her elbows. Gabrielle was enraged. How *dare* she?! Who did she think she was?! She was NOT going to get Gabrielle's ice cream! Without stopping to think, Gabrielle took a few steps backward and then launched herself at the arrogant woman's back. Her arms wound around the woman's neck and the two tumbled to the floor, scattering the crowd at Freezer #11 and creating an untidy disturbance. The woman was no meek pussycat and she began pummelling Gabrielle with her fists, at which point the store manager raced in to the fray and, with the help of several traumatized bystanders, separated the two combatants.

Gabrielle felt blood running down her face and onto the ballet pink shirt she was wearing. Naturally, it belonged to Gray. He was going to hit the roof! Mink Lady smugly straightened her hair stared in disgust at the blood dripping off the end of her right sleeve. She turned to the manager, curled her lip and announced that since she had been attacked in his store he was definitely going to be hearing from her lawyers. She demanded compensation. The manager looked from the fur coat to the bloodied nose, pulled out his cell phone and called the police.

Chastened, the ice cream shoppers returned to their quest and Gabrielle and the woman were escorted to the manager's office to await the long arm of the law. Gabrielle felt frightened and heartsick. Mink Lady pointedly ignored her and continued her tirade against the store manager. His floors were filthy. His signage was pathetic. His clientele was low-class. He had put her through trials and tribulations that she had never thought she would have to endure. And had she mentioned her lawyers? She turned to Gabrielle and pointed one long witchy finger in her direction.

"And YOU are going to jail!" she said with finality.

Gabrielle had had enough. All her life she had lived in fear. Fear of what people might think or say or do to her. Fear of the unknown, fear of the known. She had lived so much in the regrets of the past and the fears of the future that she had never found herself seated in the joys of the Now. She had rerun every negative experience she'd ever had over and over in her head so many times that they were as real today as they had been two or seven or 18 years ago. She had worried so much about what was going to happen next that she had given herself ulcers and headaches and indigestion. What about the present moment? Where had that fit into her thinking? Where had that fit into any of the thousands of negative moments that flourished in her heart every single day?

Was she leaving any room at all for happiness? Had she given all her time away to worries and dread? Was that why Gray didn't want to marry her?

Gabrielle thought about the attack this woman had launched on her ice cream and the other shoppers and decided it was time to take a stand. A stand against domineering people and her own crippling fear.

Gathering all of her courage up inside the little curve at the base of her back, Gabrielle stood up and put her hands on her hips. She jutted her chin out in front of her like the prow of a warship about to attack. And she walked over to Mink Lady and planted her fresh youthful face right in front of Mink Lady's ghastly painted one.

"Listen up, Buttercup," she spat. "You are a bully. You are a domineering insensitive cow and you've broken my nose. You want to talk about jail? I'm laying assault charges against you and calling all my friends at the newspaper to tell them to splash your picture all over town so the whole world knows how mean and miserable you are.

Now on a roll, Gabrielle added: "I've been shopping at this store for three years now and I have consistently enjoyed the experience until you showed up here today. This nice store manager doesn't want your kind in here."

Gabrielle felt intensely proud of herself. The woman looked at her through narrowed eyes and tossed her head.

"We'll see about that," she said.

When all the dust had settled and the legalities of two competing assault charges had been put to rest, Gabrielle was cleared of all charges and Mink Lady had to pay damages to both Gabrielle and the store. Gabrielle had won a massive victory. Nine ice cream-loving witnesses had come to her defense. Gabrielle didn't actually have friends in the news business but the local paper picked up her story anyway and turned her into a hero, of sorts. She'd been sticking up for the rights of the downtrodden, the newspaper reporter said. She had so many media interviews and job offers lined up it was going to take her weeks to get to them all. If not months. For the first time in her life, Gabrielle felt sure of herself. Sure of her future. She had a national following now. The possibilities were endless.

As she travelled home from the court house on the day of the trial, she found that the flush of success blooming inside her was giving her confidence to make some new decisions as well. It was time to enjoy life in the moments it occurred, she realized, not borrow worries from past and future events she could never control. In fact, it was time to take a look at that word, "control," and apply it to her life. It was time to make a few changes, strike out in a few new directions. Maybe she would study law or move to Vancouver.

Gray was sitting at the kitchen table nursing a beer and staring at a little blue velvet box sitting on the table in front of him when she walked in the front door.

He looked resigned and despondent. Gabrielle felt a rush of pity for him. He hadn't signed up for life with a celebrity. In fact, he hadn't signed up for life with a fearless woman who didn't back down from challenges.

Gabrielle smiled.

"Gray," she said. He looked up at her with a small, scared smile on his face. "I'm moving out," she said simply. Gray didn't budge. But he did start breathing again. Gabrielle gave him a hug.

"You're a good guy," she said. Want to help me pack?"

Gray stared at her for a long time before speaking.

"You're the boss," he said finally.

"You bet I am," Gabrielle smiled.

"Can I call you some time?" Gray said.

"We'll see," said Gabrielle. "We'll see."

Marla's Miracle

Marla sighed and blew her bangs out of her eyes for what seemed like the thousandth time since breakfast. Blasted hair. Jake loved it this way but she was tired of looking through a dark brown fringe all the time. It made her feel cloistered into a monastery or something; it kept her from feeling like an active part of a vibrant world.

She ran the cold water for a few minutes before filling the kettle. Jake insisted his tea be made from cold water. He said there was more oxygen in cold water and it helped him think better. What exactly he needed to think about Marla wasn't sure. He was an accountant. He counted. Money, mostly, but how much thinking was really required when all you had to do was add and subtract — with a calculator for heaven's sake! Jake followed the rules of accounting to the letter, ensuring those small columns of numbers stood in straight rigid rows on the page. Deviation was neither admired nor allowed.

He was like that with most things, Marla mused. Towels stacked in the linen cupboard? Straight rigid rows. Glasses on the kitchen shelf? Straight and rigid. Socks and underwear? You guessed it.

The only apparent exception to Jake's mania for tidiness was Marla's bangs. Whenever she went to the hairdresser he would spend weeks beforehand pleading with her to keep her bangs long. Marla's bangs had been exactly the same length since the day Jake had clapped eyes on her and, frankly, she was getting tired of them. Way PAST tired of them. It was time for a change.

Their marriage had been a reasonably successful one, as marriages go, Marla decided. She had never actually felt deliriously happy with the match she had made, but Jake had been a good man, if a little dull. He didn't drink, didn't smoke and he never went "out with the boys." What's more, the crummy old car he insisted on driving wasn't going to send the family to the poor house any time soon. He loved repairing the old junker, and the hours he spent in the garage with his tools and cans of oil meant Marla didn't have to hear him complaining about anything – like the length of her bangs.

She sighed and put the kettle on the burner. And that was another thing: What was wrong with an electric kettle for a change? Why did she always have to heat the water up so slowly on the top of the stove? Didn't he think she might have other things to do than stand and watch the kettle boil? Stove top kettles were a fire hazard — Marla had read that in The Reader's Digest a few years ago — but Jake wouldn't hear of getting an electric one.

"Tea won't taste as good," he'd said tersely.

What made him such a blooming expert on tea, she wondered? Marla had seen a beautiful new kettle advertised in the most recent issue of Architectural Digest and she was aching to bring one home. It was stunning. And it was electric. Would Jake even notice the difference? She spent her entire life waiting on him hand and foot but he barely noticed. Marla just knew an expensive new designer kettle would improve the quality of Jake's tea. The fact that she could tell all her friends that she had one would be just the icing on the cake.

While she waited for the kettle to boil, Marla organized cups, milk and sugar and rooted around in the cupboard for a tray to put them on. Sometimes she wished she didn't have to put up with Jake and his selfish ways. Sometimes she wished he would drop out of her life so she could start over. She sighed again. Why did he always have to say "No?"

Marla wiped the tea tray and popped a chocolate truffle into her mouth. She kept them hidden in the pot drawer so Jake wouldn't find them and eat them all himself. It was a small victory for her, she thought: so far he hadn't stumbled onto her stash. And it was also a mercy that she'd been able to talk him into the new kitchen renovation last year — otherwise she wouldn't have a nice pot drawer to use as a treasure chest! Marla ran her hand along the top of the gleaming granite countertop and smiled at the top-of-the-line appliances standing guard over her kitchen. She's had to fight tooth and nail to get them – she'd even had to threaten Jake, playfully of course, that she would leave him if he wouldn't do this one little thing for her.

Wheedling the new kitchen out of her tightwad husband had been a sweet triumph for her but Marla couldn't understand why Jake never bothered to come and make his own tea from time to time. He was too busy writing articles for the accounting association journal he was so manic about. She was beginning to suspect it was his way of avoiding her.

"Make me a cup of tea, would you Babe?" he'd asked airily just now. Right when she was on her way out to check the mail. There might be something interesting in the mail today, something for *her* for a change. It wasn't as though she didn't have important things to do herself, for pity's sake. She had her bowling league every Monday afternoon and she went shopping with Jennie Martin from down the street every other Thursday. Wednesday was her day to shop — the flyers came out every Wednesday and she liked to get to the specials early — and of course Fridays she got her hair done. She had become very fond of the new salon in town and although it was a hideously expensive place for a wash and set, they served champagne to all their Friday customers and she felt she deserved a few perks in life. After all, Jake was probably going to get a new car next year. You could buy an awful lot of haircuts for the price of a new car!

And the sacrifices she had made for her family! The kids were grown now and they were busy in ways that no longer included their mother. How had that happened? One day she was in demand 24 hours a day and suddenly, it seemed, they were gone, embraced by the challenges of a bigger world. They were both still quite close to their father for some reason, and Marla was a little jealous of the fact that they always spent longer on the phone with Jake than they did with her. That wasn't really fair. She was the one who had given birth and warmed most of the bottles. Jake? All he seemed to do was listen.

Jake had been pretty good at driving the kids places, though, she conceded. Marilyn had been a soccer nut and Warren had played hockey all the time. Thank goodness Jake didn't mind watching all those boring games! Marla drew the line at sports. She didn't mind cooking and laundry but she was certainly not going to spend her life in a hockey arena! In fact, if she had known how much work raising children was before she'd signed up for the project she wasn't sure she would have jumped in. It had been an exhausting few decades!

Marla squared her shoulders defiantly. She deserved a little free time now, time to read and drink coffee with her friends.

Funny that she never seemed to have a lot of time to do all that fun stuff, though. The house always needed a little tidying and she was partial to a few TV shows that she just hated to miss – especially now that she had finally convinced Jake to get that new high definition big screen TV. It wasn't as big as the one Jennie Martin had just bought, but it didn't embarrass her too badly, most of the time. It would do for now.

Yes, Marla sighed, it was tough enough trying to fit everything in to an average day without stopping to make a cup of tea at a moment's notice. Who did Jake think he was? And why was he working at home so much lately anyway? The guy had barely passed his 53rd birthday – he was way too young to retire. Jake had kept himself in reasonable shape over the years but he had become wheezy. The noise of his breathing was very distracting. Marla hated sharing her space with people.

And the issue of her hair. Marla never understood why it meant so much to Jake that she keep it long but here was yet another way she had to put aside her own inclinations and cater to the man she had married. Didn't he understand how much she sacrificed for him?

There had been a time when men thought Marla was a bit of a dish – of course that was before she'd gained so much weight, but that wasn't really her fault – having babies just wrecks a gal's figure, everybody knew that. Her hair used to sway down her back in a cascade of brown velvet and she'd kept her bangs short, never even close to grazing her eyebrows. Along came Jake and suddenly he was pressuring her to keep the fringe long all the time, just like some pouty movie star.

Thank goodness for their bargain, Marla thought smugly: if a month passed and she didn't cut her bangs above her eyebrows, Jake had to hand her enough cash for a new outfit.

It was important that she dress nicely, she had argued. She was an accountant's wife, after all, and appearances were important. Jake never bothered getting new clothes of his own – he looked dreadful all the time and it was downright embarrassing to be seen in public with him.

Marla had come close to cutting her bangs short numerous times but Jennie had said long bangs made her look thinner so she gave in to Jake's badgering and left them alone. When she got a job again, though, she'd have to do something about them – they just weren't tidy.

Marla had been thinking about getting a job for quite a few years now. At first she'd thought she'd go back to work when the kids started school but she was quite surprised at how time-consuming their school careers were for her.

She had to make lunches and supervise the homework and they seemed to need school supplies all the time. How on Earth did working mothers manage to pull in a pay cheque and still be decent parents? Marla just knew it couldn't be done.

Marla had also thought of starting a career when Marilyn finally joined her older brother at university. But it had been such a relief to finally have a few minutes to herself, she just hadn't gotten around to doing anything about it. And the house took so much of her time, too, that it was impossible to fit a job search into her schedule.

And then there was the little question of what to put on her résumé. Marla had a college degree in psychology and she'd done some filing at a human resources company after graduation for a few months. That still rankled. Who did they think they were, making a college graduate do their filing for them every day? She really deserved something more impressive, so she'd left that job and started looking for something better. That something appeared to be Jake, at least in the beginning.

The two had married, started a family and poof! More than 20 years had gone by before Marla could think seriously about tackling the workforce again. Maybe she'd go back to school one of these days and retrain. She liked reading. Maybe she would become a librarian.

Marla treated herself to another truffle while she thought about becoming a librarian. It was an agreeable thought, sitting there all day surrounded by books and quiet people. She was pretty sure she would get a good long lunch break every day. And the library would be closed Sundays so she wouldn't have to work on Sundays.

There might be the odd Saturday shift as well, but that would be OK because then she wouldn't have to listen to Jake muttering in the garage all day as he tried to patch up his old Ford sedan.

Marla really wished Jake *would* get himself a decent car. It was embarrassing to wheel her little BMW convertible into the driveway and leave it standing beside Jake's old pile of junk. Every time she mentioned it to him he would just sigh and look at her from behind those fuddy-duddy glasses of his.

"We can't afford *your* car, Marla, how on Earth would we ever find the money for a new one for me?"

Marla thought that was a bit dramatic. She had bought the BMW on a whim, as a present to herself on her 47th birthday. She had been feeling a little sad that she was growing older without the compensations of a big house on the lake or a vacation home in Europe.

A new car was just the thing to lift her spirits. And it did! Too bad Jake wasn't a kindred spirit when it came to cars. She could just imagine what the other librarians would say when they saw her leaving the parking lot in her shiny BMW. Oh my, that would make her feel good!

In the meantime there was Jake and his darned tea to drag around the house. The kettle boiled and Marla splashed some hot water into the teapot to warm it up, then dumped the water into the gold-trimmed china mugs she'd bought barely a month ago. She had 12 complete place settings hidden away in the basement but she hadn't had the nerve to bring them out to show Jake just yet. Two mugs were bold enough for now.

The dishes had cost an unholy fortune and Jake would most certainly launch into his boring lecture about her spending habits if more dishes suddenly started appearing in the china cabinet. All Jake ever seemed to do was complain about her spending, Marla griped to herself. What a cheapskate. She was entitled to a few treats now and then, wasn't she?

While the tea was steeping Marla stepped out onto the front porch to pull a tangle of envelopes out of the mailbox. She hadn't yet made the leap to email so the daily postal delivery was important – it was her connection to a bigger world.

Today's assortment of mail included the usual litter of flyers and the annoying clutch of bills that never seemed to stop arriving. She would hand those over to Jake with his tea – bills were not her concern. Maybe a pool company had an insert in today's flyers, though – it was time to get a bigger one, she thought. Just the thing to dream about over a nice cup of tea. Her first soap of the day would be on in a few minutes as well. It was time to take a break.

Marla turned back into the house, sorting mail with polished efficiency as she walked past the set of bronze sculptures she'd bought last spring for the front hallway. They needed dusting, she thought absent-mindedly as she walked into the kitchen. She'd have to get after the cleaning lady about that.

As Marla reached the centre island of her beautiful new kitchen, a large fat envelope dropped to the floor with a thud. She picked it up and stared aghast at the return address. "Bankruptcy Court," it said. Marla's heart started beating faster. Alarmed, she checked the timer. Two minutes more and a perfect cup of tea would be ready.

What had Jake done now? Opening the envelope, Marla read documents confirming that Jake's application for bankruptcy had been legally approved. The bum had gone bankrupt!

The tea timer went off but Marla didn't stop to feel annoyed or pour the tea – she raced out of the kitchen and through her perfectly organized living room, with its leather couches and Persian carpets, and on into Jake's study. Her hands shook and her heart thumped – how *dare* he go bankrupt. He hadn't even told her he was thinking about it!

"Jake Milton what the devil have you been up to?" she roared as she neared the battered old eyesore of a desk he'd been using since university. Jake, lounging back in his chair with his eyes open in surprise, didn't blink. Marla hit him on the shoulder with the hand that held the letter and shook it at him.

"What is this all about?" she screamed in his face. Jake still didn't blink. In fact, he didn't move. Marla poked his stomach.

"I'm talking to you!" she yelled. Jake didn't budge. Marla stepped back a little and stared in disbelief at the body that had once belonged to her husband; she gaped at how pathetic it looked, frozen grimly in the agony of death. How dare he end it all this way!

Marla called 911 to order the emergency services people to remove her husband's body and she was on the phone angrily booking a hair appointment when they arrived. The paramedics gently examined what remained of Jake and turned to comfort his wife.

"What did he die from?" Marla asked impatiently as they prepared to move Jake out of her house. She felt she'd been having a very hard day and was eager to get on with the formalities so she could figure out what on Earth to do next with her life.

The lead paramedic looked at Jake's scuffed shoes and shabby sweater, his tired office furnishings and his immaculate, cheerless wife.

"Heart failure," he said shortly.

Marla stared at the man and thought of her bleak future. It had never occurred to her to worry about Jake's heart.

"I guess I'd better get my heart checked as soon as possible!" She exclaimed. What if she had a heart defect too?!

The man took in Marla's beautiful clothes and her carefully manicured hands. He noticed the hole in Jake's sweater and the piece of tape holding his eyeglasses together. He couldn't help noticing the letter still clutched in Marla's hand, the one with the word "Bankrupt" written across the top in large letters. He'd seen this story before. It made him sad.

"I'd say that's a good idea, ma'am," he said quietly. "Maybe it's not too late."

Marla turned and looked at the man. She felt suddenly smaller, vulnerable even.

"Maybe it's not," she said. "Maybe it's not."

Charlie's Choice

A Short Story

Charlie looked up at the cloudless blue sky above her head and stretched her arms up to their limit, thankful for another peaceful day. She wiggled her ankles from side to side to dig her bare feet deeper into the cool sand of spring and stood there for a moment, breathing in the fishy smell of the rippling lake water. She was a little lonely, truth be told, a little sad.

A gentle whine interrupted Charlie's thoughts and she looked down at the sodden black lab at her side.

"Oh Trooper, am I forgetting you?" she asked. The dog cocked his head and looked expectantly up at her, his tongue hanging out of a mouth that was ringed with sand. He was still panting from his last chase in the lake and he was eager for more.

Charlie picked up the thick black stick at her feet and flung it back into the water, labouring a little to send it farther this time, and the lab immediately rocketed out into the water to fetch it. Trooper could play stick for hours.

Later they would sit on Charlie's beachfront porch and watch the clouds and gulls get ready for sunset, and later still they would ignore the sand between their toes as they drifted off to sleep in Charlie's antique four-poster. They would have made new memories like the old ones and the sun would rise again.

But Charlie had other things on her mind today and lovely as tired dogs and sandy sheets were, she needed to focus on her future. Unmarried at 40 and childless, she belonged to that unsung army of women who have reached a stage in life where they understand, suddenly and for all time – sooner than others perhaps – that they are Alone.

The anguish and chaos of tidying away the evidence of her parents' lives had been hard on Charlie and it seemed like just a heartbeat since they had passed out of her life. There had been bills to pay and accounts to close, property to sell and furniture to disperse. Like so many other orphaned adults, she had held on to far too many of her parents' possessions, hoping to stay connected to their memories through the things they had loved best.

Charlie's parents had not been wealthy people and it wasn't in the family way to talk about money. But decades ago they had bought a little beachfront house some miles west of Port Stanley, Ontario, and it had given them unending delight. The house was Charlie's now.

"Trooper, sit," she said. Trooper looked up at his mistress quizzically and pranced a little before parking his rear on the water-spotted sand. "I need to talk to you," Charlie said.

Trooper looked at Charlie and then at the stick. He loved Charlie whole-heartedly and it didn't matter to him that she sometimes ate ice cream right out of the container, or failed to clean up the dinner dishes. He didn't notice that the zipper on her size 12 trousers was in danger of splitting or that gray roots sometimes shone through the pretty ginger colour of her hair. She gave a good scratch, that woman. He was a happy dog.

"We need to make a decision," Charlie was saying. She felt brave and scared, all at the same time. Trooper listened attentively.

"I've got a job offer, Trooper," she began. "My boss thinks I'm a shoe-in for one of the branch manager's jobs that's just opened up in Toronto. It would be a huge promotion."

Trooper panted and waited.

"It would be awfully exciting," she said. We'd finally get to break out of small town life. That's what I've always wanted, isn't it?

Trooper didn't know. And now, perched on the edge of the biggest decision of her life, neither did Charlie. She had been finishing her degree in finance when she had fallen in love with the carefree Jake Brissom, a divorced man seven years older than her and one whose two children arrived at his home every other weekend for their legal allotment of time with their father. They were both under the age of seven and initially Jake had said he was concerned about moving a woman into their lives so soon after the divorce.

A few years later he had said he was worried about commitment. Charlie had invested five years of her life with Jake and his family before deciding she either had to move in with the man or move on. Having been stung once in marriage, Jake had explained, he just couldn't take another chance.

It took all Charlie's courage to break away from him – after all, she loved him -- but this was about pride and she wanted more from a relationship than Jake was offering. Six months later, she cried for hours when she found out he was engaged to that awful Sarah Blunden who worked at the St. Thomas Y.

Meanwhile, Charlie's best friend Marsha Jones had landed a job as a lawyer in a downtown Toronto law firm, and she had swept into big city life with passion and verve. Charlie enviously listened to Marsha's news about the concerts, restaurants and fitness clubs that filled her days, and the succession of men rotating through Marsha's life had been impressive. Eventually Marsha married and brought two sweet little children into a life of comfort.

Almost as soon as Jake withered off her horizon, Charlie's mother had been diagnosed with the lingering intestinal disease that eventually extinguished her. Before Charlie really had the energy to take wing and fly to Toronto -- where she had always thought she *should* be living -- she thrust herself into the role of caregiver and spent all her available time driving her mother to

doctors' appointments or helping keep her parent's bungalow clean and neat. She had made meals for her parents and tended their garden. She had fussed over her father's failing eyesight and completed his tax returns.

And although she was a willing worker in the project, Charlie thought with some regret about the brilliant future she had always wanted, one that would take her away from London and St. Thomas and their ebbing main streets, and off to a world of bustle and commerce. Instead of working diligently at a London bank and going to bed early every Friday night, maybe she could be at the helm of a busy

Toronto bank branch and wearing saucy little dresses to swanky parties. Or maybe not. But it might be nice to have that choice.

No, Charlie hadn't planned to devote 10 years of her life to her parents' needs but like most things in life, days bled into weeks and weeks collected into months and eventually, like a raindrop threading its way through streams and creeks, lakes and rivers, Charlie floated her way to a distant ocean of life a decade beyond her starting point. Her mother's end had been an easy one, and Charlie felt blessed to have been there for it. She was exhausted.

Charlie might have set off for Toronto at that point to bring a brilliant future to life in that mysterious world of glass towers and littered streets, but she had chosen to stay: her father had needed her help transitioning to a smaller life in an empty house. Three lonely New Year's Eves passed her by. With her father's death, Charlie had been just too worn out to think about making any changes. In fact, she had decided she didn't need to. She was too old for a big city life now.

All those years of patient caretaking, those years of watching hope for her future dim one tiny mirage at a time, they'd all been worth it, in a sad way, and she had her cottage on the beach as compensation. Why did the district manager of her bank have to ruin it all now by pushing her towards the branch manager's job that had cropped up in an area of Toronto they called "The Beach?" Charlie liked the sound of that name – it felt like home. But she already had a home.

"You're perfect for the job, Charlie," Rick had told her, his excitement finding no answering resonance in her heart.

Rick was on his second marriage and he seemed stained by optimism.

Charlie wasn't so sure she wanted a perfect job in the City anymore. She already managed a successful bank branch half an hour away in London. Her successes there had often brought her to the attention of that nebulous place they call Head Office. She had finally succeeded in organizing her life so that everything was predictable and safe. Toronto was full of nightmare traffic problems and random murders – how could anyone plan a decent life in a city like that?

No, Charlie was beyond adventure now, beyond the silvery reach of big dreams and star-struck hopes for a brighter tomorrow. She was firmly entrenched in a predictable life in a relatively safe community. She had security now. Wasn't that enough?

Well, wasn't it?

A little flicker of curiosity scintillated down Charlie's backbone and Marsha's excited urging prompted her to take a look at what she was passing up.

"Come for a weekend at least," Marsha had said on the phone the night before. "We'll have a blast!"

Charlie felt she was too old to use words like "blast." But she wasn't yet too old for a weekend in the City and she would like to see Marsha and her family again. Charlie packed a bag, dropped Trooper off at her cousin's house in Iona Station and took a deep breath.

She took the train to Toronto so she wouldn't have to worry about dangerous items flying off trucks on the highway. She had bought a personal safety alarm and she had stashed her money securely around her waist in a money belt in case she was robbed as she made her way to Marsha's office.

She might be a small town girl at heart but she was no fool.

As the train made its way into the downtown core, Charlie marvelled at how big the buildings were – and how they seemed to be crammed into as little space as possible. She had been to Toronto several years earlier – or was it a decade ago? – and she had forgotten how busy it was.

"Too many people," she sniffed. Her heart beat faster.

The train station was packed with people who all seemed in a terrible hurry to get somewhere else but Charlie was in no hurry at all. She wasn't due to meet Marsha for hours yet.

"Why can't they all just relax?" she wondered, wrapping her best spring jacket more tightly around her for comfort. She noticed most of the women were wearing spiky heels and she was regretting her sensible choice of shoes.

Charlie's new jeans and sweater, which had seemed so practical in the Wal-Mart dressing room, now felt uncomfortable next to her skin as she noticed the nice suits and skimpy skirts of the women who were racing through the station with so much certainty.

Marsha had given Charlie detailed directions on how to get to her office building through the underground tunnels that led from Union Station. She was headed towards a building called "First Canadian Place." Navigating her way through the maze of shopping opportunities and rushing people was a nightmare but she saw some gorgeous clothes she might like to try on. Later, maybe. Another time. Another year. There would be another opportunity. Wouldn't there?

Wouldn't there?

Charlie stopped in front of a brilliantly lit store window and gazed at the smart gray suits on the mannequins before her. Five gray suits, each one unique, were all accessorized with pretty blouses and sparkling jewelry. Off to the side was one mannequin in a daring red suit that had been paired with a tight black scoop-neck camisole. It looked fresh and exciting by comparison.

Even though London had large stores and affluent shoppers, Charlie had always thought it was a city that actually had very little to offer. Very little choice. Even as the thought formed in her head, Charlie realized the words applied to almost everything in her life right now: So little choice.

She stood and stared at the red suit for a long time, frowning slightly and trying to look more worldly than she felt. Finally, she gathered up her courage and walked into the store, "just to look" she told herself. Clothes had never seemed important to her before.

An eager young salesgirl, focused on a new commission, smiled brightly and offered to help.

"No thanks, just looking," Charlie said casually. Just looking, she thought. Always looking. Always looking after someone or looking behind at sad memories. The salesgirl was dressed in a snug brown pencil skirt and a cream-coloured Lycra top. She wore four-inch heels and Charlie wondered how she could stand all day without toppling over. The shoes made Charlie nervous. The sales girl smiled and swept an appraising glance Charlie's way.

"You'd look good in green," she said, pointing to a rack in the middle of the store. Charlie liked green and went over to look. The salesgirl was too pretty and too skinny, she thought, although the green *had* been a good suggestion.

The rack held a row of beautiful Kelly green skirts and jackets and Charlie knew she would never have the nerve to try any of them on. Besides, she didn't really need new clothes. Looking was a good idea, though – she had to do something with her time. She thought about how even being in Toronto right now felt like a dramatic departure from Reality. Her life had become entirely predictable and there was never any variation in it, from the bowl of Corn Flakes she ate every morning for breakfast to the 28-minute route she took every day to work.

Charlie liked predictability. And as she looked at the beautiful green suits on the rack in a well-lit store in a strange city, it suddenly occurred to her that the future as she was now creating it might end up looking exactly like the past she had just finished living. She had never seen a kelly green suit anywhere in St. Thomas or London and when she returned to her little house by the Courthouse, there would be no green suits hanging in her closet, either.

Charlie suddenly saw, with absolute clarity and terror, that the future she would face if she stayed where she was in life would hold no variation or distinction, it would be neither hopeful nor beautiful, shining nor strange.

Once upon a time she had been young and vibrant, energetic and optimistic. She had seen possibilities where none existed and she had been absolutely determined to grab hold of the world around her and bend it to her will. Once upon a time, she had planned a life that would be full of dinners out and trips abroad, promotions at work and children's toys left scattered around the family room floor. If she had known about them at the time, she probably would have wanted to fill her future with green suits as well.

What had happened to that girl? Charlie ran a finger along the textured weave of cloth on a rack and frowned. Perhaps it was love's fault, she thought. Her exuberant love for Jake had led her to cast aside her dreams of moving to this awful and wonderful city and devote herself to his every need – and those of his children.

Her devoted love for her parents had led her to cast aside her dreams for a brilliant future yet again and accompany them on a passage to another life, one that didn't include her. Yet. Trooper would one day pass out of her life as well. What was left for her to love anymore? Charlie suddenly felt depleted.

She gave the skinny salesgirl a frozen smile and walked dejectedly out of the store. Across the shopping corridor a trendy coffee shop beckoned and she went in and ordered the least intimidating coffee on the menu.

Charlie sat down, her little wheeled weekend suitcase at her side, her frayed leather purse perched safely on her lap. As she waited for her coffee to cool she watched the parade of people bustling past, deep in lives that seemed important and vast. She thought that most of them were probably ignorant about Death, and how it rattles in to claim us by inches and surprise.

Charlie was an expert on Death. There was no point fighting against its arrival, no point pretending it wasn't there waiting to invite us beyond the veiled mirage of activity we frenetically label Life. Whether it was throwing sticks to a beloved dog on a beach or tottering through underground corridors on towering heels, we are all ignoring our end in one way or another, she thought.

Was that why Charlie didn't want to move to Toronto? Because all that was left for her to do in this world was to wait for her turn to die?

Or was it possible that there might be a lot Charlie didn't know about Life? Was it possible that *she* was the ignorant one? A little slice of window far above Charlie's head opened onto the street level outside and she caught a glimpse of a man walking by leading a beautiful golden retriever on a sparkling metal leash. The dog looked happy. There seemed to be a lot of good sniffing to be done out on that street.

Charlie sat at the little round table she had claimed, with her cooling coffee and her fear of living, and wrestled with the confusing emotions that flooded over her. Something had changed now. Something strange and uncomfortable had floated into her heart and she wasn't sure what to do with it. What now?

Long after her coffee had been reduced to a cold wet rim around the bottom of a paper cup, Charlie stood up and walked thoughtfully out of the coffee shop. She threaded her way through the torrent of people bubbling through the corridor and landed in front of the suit store yet again.

She looked at the gray suits with their colourful blouses and she glanced at the red outfit with its daring black top.

After a few more moments she walked into the store and over to the rack of Kelly green suits, and she smiled slightly at the skinny salesgirl who was hovering hopefully near the jewelry counter.

"Going to try something?" Skinny asked.

Charlie nodded, understanding finally dawning on her.

"I think it's time to try just about everything," Charlie said slowly.

Skinny nodded knowingly.

"It doesn't hurt to try," she said.

Charlie nodded her head.

"Maybe not," she said.

Planning for Partnership

A Short Story

Deirdre wrestled her carry-on bag up the crowded aisle and silently cursed the people standing in her way. She had a lot of reading to do on this trip and she needed to get at it.

It was a crime she couldn't fly first class anymore. What was with that anyway? It was so unfair. So what if billings at the law firm she worked at were down substantially this year? The *partners* still flew first class. She worked at least as hard as any one of them, and what did she get? A cramped window-seat in the back of the red-eye.

She shook her head in disgust as she found her seat and stashed her bag on the floor in front of her. Deirdre didn't carry a purse anymore as it branded her a female and she didn't want her clients to think of her as a woman. In any sense of the word. Her dirty blonde hair was pulled back in a practical ponytail and secured with no-nonsense clips, and her dark sensible shoes were a perfect match for her expensive navy blue pin-striped pantsuit. She hated jewelry but she did wear a sturdy Rolex watch that she had bought to celebrate her 35th birthday last year.

It was a very nice watch.

Deirdre was not a classically beautiful woman, at least not in her own mind, but she had a finely sculpted face that would be agreeable if it weren't posed in quite so harsh a configuration all the time. She didn't care about beauty anymore, although she did bend enough to wear a pale shade of lipstick most of the time. It kept her lips from drying out.

She pulled out the first brief she was expected to read and glanced at her beautiful, chunky watch to take note of the time. This was billable work and she wanted credit for every minute.

By the time she got to Toronto she needed to finish her reading and develop a strategy for handling the meeting ahead – the legal team for a large Toronto corporation was going to be watching her every move and she needed to be ready with an answer to every question they asked. In fact she needed to be ready for every question they didn't ask as well, and that was probably the harder task at hand.

A lot was riding on this meeting. It was an opportunity that had come up out of the blue and she had jumped on the chance to head east on behalf of her firm. If all went well, she would land another plum client and her value to the firm would escalate yet again. She would continue to ride the elevator up to full partnership and there was no end of perks waiting for her there. A corner office. Her name on the stationery. Free parking in the garage. A bigger expense account.

She counted the blessings partnership would confer and smiled smugly as she thought of the other women at Bailey and Bell Barristers and Solicitors Ltd. The mothers, especially. They were all hampered by relationships and commitments, children and nannies and every single one of them needed time off every now and then. Every one of them suffered from a litany of problems and obstacles to partnership that Deirdre didn't have to endure. She was free and dedicated. Everybody knew that. Everybody admired her. Or should.

Deirdre had started her legal career with a great deal of enthusiasm and an unlimited rainbow of hope for her future. Graduating at the top of her class she had landed a coveted articling position with Bailey and Bell. She had worked 100-hour weeks and taken up golf so she could spend time with the important people who might become her clients. She had worked her way on to the boards of several charitable organizations so she could increase her credibility as well as her client base. She even volunteered for the University of Calgary Law School alumni organization just so everyone would know how important and selfless she was.

Deirdre was a raving success in her chosen field and her billings were consistently strong.

She smiled grimly. The bonus had better be good this year. She wanted a bigger condo and a new car. She wanted a membership at that new private club that had opened up in town. Maybe she'd get some investment diamonds, too. If she was going to work this hard, she needed reminders that it was all worth it. Deirdre needed a few perks.

It was a shame she had missed every important family celebration that had taken place over the past seven years and, to be honest, she couldn't even remember the last time she had had a date. Holidays? She was pretty sure she had been to Curaçao last winter.

There had been a time when Deirdre had thought she was headed for a life of ease. She had been in love, way back in her undergrad years, and she had been ready to commit herself completely to a future with Tommy Johnson. At the time she had thought he was everything a man should be – strong, handsome, intelligent and fun. He was a business student and he was active in student affairs. He was good to his mother and his sisters. He treated Deirdre like a princess and, in the beginning, he had said he believed that after they got married and started having children, Deirdre should have the right to choose what she wanted to do in life: work, stay home, whatever. It didn't matter. Somehow they would manage. Deirdre thought she might want to work part-time. Three kids would be perfect.

Deirdre sighed as she thought of Tommy's green eyes and bright red hair. He had been tall, a characteristic she admired in a man. She was still bitter about the breakup.

Tommy was two years older than Deirdre and it was no surprise to her when he sailed off to Law School. It was what he had always wanted to do, what he was perfectly suited for in life. But Deirdre thought it had changed him.

He became more serious, less carefree. He began spending more time with his law school friends and less time watching movies and cooking dinner with Deirdre. They stopped hiking together and he even forgot her birthday. He said he was sorry — law school was his biggest priority. Couldn't she understand for once? Deirdre didn't like his tone.

Tommy's opinions began to change, too. Where once he had thought he didn't care what a life partner did with her time, he began to believe Deirdre should stay home with their children after they began to arrive. He was going to need a lot of support if he was going to succeed in law. It's not that women were "supposed" to look after the home front exactly. It's just that it was probably better for everybody if that's what his woman did. Deirdre wasn't so sure that was what was best for her. Did she have to decide right now?

There were other problems, too. Tommy wished she would wear more makeup. He didn't like her laugh. He thought she was too intellectual. Deirdre slowly realized the joy had gone out of their relationship and she watched as the passion drained out of their love one sweet droplet at a time until she woke up one morning and realized she no longer wanted to lie in his arms or laugh at his jokes.

She didn't feel excited when he dragged himself home in the small hours of the morning after a night at the library. She wasn't sure he was even glad to come home to her any more. They were, however, still a couple, and she wanted to make it all work.

And she would have, too, except that Tommy began spending time with an undergrad by the name of Shelley. Shelley was very pretty and she giggled a lot. She smelled of lilacs and peppermint. She wore lots of makeup and spent her spare time knitting (who knits anymore?). Deirdre didn't know how Tommy had met her, exactly, but she did know she was seeing them walking together on campus a lot. It was when she saw Tommy landing a gentle peck on Shelley's cheek that Deirdre decided she'd had enough.

Tommy was relieved to confront the issue.

"She knows she doesn't want to work," Tommy said simply.

Deirdre applied to law school that very afternoon. Eventually Tommy married Shelley and at last report, they had two sweet children, a cottage near Canmore and a large vacation home in Arizona. Shelley, of course, was too busy being a housewife to work. Apparently she had taken up horseback riding and figure skating. Deirdre shuddered at the thought of Tommy and Shelley hiding out in their cozy little domesticated life. It struck her as being small and inconsequential.

From what she had seen, marriage was over-rated any way. She had a fast car, a large, beautifully furnished condo downtown and the respect of her peers. That was enough for her.

Shelley, by comparison, really only had Tommy.

Life was pretty good, all in all. Deirdre felt important. Lately another lawyer in her firm had taken to stopping by her office to chat and Deirdre found the attention puzzling. Jared was nice looking and all, and he had a nice smile. He worked very, very hard and his conversation was always fairly interesting. He had suggested they go for drinks sometime. But Deirdre didn't need a man. She didn't need anyone anymore. Drinks? She drank alone at home.

A frumpy middle-aged woman in jeans and a grimy blue sweat top lumbered down the aisle and squeezed into the seat beside Deirdre. She fastened her seat belt. Deirdre groaned inwardly. Great. Another chatty housewife to endure. She glanced at the woman's jeans and oversized sweat top and guessed they came from Wal-Mart. She was grateful she didn't have to shop there. Truth to tell, she didn't even know where to find one.

The woman leaned back in her chair and looked at Deirdre. She smiled warmly.

"Oh my God I miss my kids already!" she said winningly. But Deirdre was not interested in conversation. She didn't have kids and she didn't want to hear about any that belonged to someone else. The woman gave up waiting for a reply and, eventually, she closed her eyes and exhaled slowly. The airplane taxied down the runway for takeoff and the woman still didn't stir; Deirdre relaxed. She hated sitting next to people who wanted to talk all the time. This one would probably want to talk non-stop about her children and her husband, her recipes for tomato soup and her knitting. There was no polite way to shut these people up; this lady might be very nice in her own small little world but she was obviously not a prospective client and Deirdre certainly didn't want to waste valuable time talking to a nobody. It sounded harsh, even to Deirdre's hardened ears, but it was the truth and she didn't need to apologize for it. Business was business.

Deirdre looked at the woman's messy hair and lined face. She guessed she'd be about 45 and although she wasn't unattractive exactly, she was no raving beauty either. The woman's hand fell over the seat divider and her head rolled uncomfortably close to Deirdre's face. Deirdre grimaced. Ugh. It was revolting, really. Who did this woman think she was?! When the woman made no move to retreat, Deirdre picked the hand up as though she were handling a slug and moved it onto the woman's lap.

Startled, the housewife opened her eyes.

"I really hate to be touched," Deirdre explained. "You were interfering with my space." There was a note of exasperation in Deirdre's voice and she didn't realize that she was flaring her nostrils and looking down her nose as she spoke.

The housewife looked puzzled for a moment and then muttered a weary "Sorry," before shrugging restlessly and closing her eyes again.

Deirdre was annoyed by the lack of deference the woman was showing her. She made a point of dressing well when she travelled – you never knew who you might meet –

and she thought it was obvious that she was working on something *important*.

That was the thing about housewives. They always seemed to believe they were as good as everybody else. They spent their time shopping and drinking coffee with their friends, watching TV and wiping dirty noses — while the *rest* of womankind contributed to the world in substantial ways. Take this lady, for example. Here she was, taking the red-eye from Calgary to Toronto on a Wednesday, dressed like a slob and flopping her body over onto other people without so much as a bow of regret. Who did she think she was?!

"Well don't let it happen again, please," Deirdre said. "I have important work to do here and I need to concentrate."

The housewife looked at her but said nothing.

"Do. You. Understand?" Deirdre added, for emphasis.

The housewife rolled her eyes and sat up. She gave Deirdre an appraising, almost pitying look as she took in her ringless fingers, her cold, starchy, appearance and the thick pile of papers in front of her. Her eyes narrowed.

"You make a lot of assumptions, little girl," the housewife said evenly but not unkindly.

Deirdre waved a hand in the woman's face to tell her to buzz off and went back to her reading.

"Oh *please*," she said.

"Please what?" the housewife asked calmly.

Her disrespectful attitude enraged Deirdre.

"Please do something valuable for society for a change. Please stop being so lazy. Please stop pretending that working women like me are pathetic and useless. Please stop getting all your value from the man you married or the children you brought into the world. I don't want to hear about your cute little kid and the drawing he made for you. I don't want to hear about your recipe for apple pie. I really don't care where you get the best price on organic fruit juice and if you are dying to tell someone about how forgetful your darling husband is then I would take it as a kindness if you would move out of that damned seat right now and go sit somewhere else.

Deirdre paused for a moment, then continued: "I have a career on the go here and I find your kind of talk incredibly boring. I have an important meeting in the morning and I need to get ready for it. You are taking me away from much more important issues. So *please* find some fashion magazine to read or something. Got it?"

Deirdre was pointing her finger in the woman's face and her own features were contorted in anger. Such a display of emotion was uncharacteristic for Deirdre but she felt much better after she had said her piece. These housewives thought they knew everything. This one didn't even have the decency to back away. Deirdre frowned and turned back to her brief.

The housewife said nothing for a moment but then tapped Deirdre on the shoulder lightly and quietly cleared her throat.

"You know, it's OK to be angry but it's really not good for you," she said. "Anger is a short cut to illness. And you know what? It's OK to love a man and have a family. It doesn't mean you're done with life."

Deirdre ignored her.

The cabin was quiet for the rest of the flight and Deirdre worked in a pool of light that illuminated little beyond the ghostly white papers she was methodically reviewing. She glanced at the woman sitting beside her a few times and felt new waves of irritation rising in her throat. No wonder she was taking the red-eye -- the fares were usually a lot cheaper and she probably couldn't afford to fly in proper daylight. That being said, the rings she was wearing had some pretty big diamonds in them. They were probably fake. It was hard to tell these days.

Deirdre sat back for a moment and thought about rings. There had been a time when she had wanted a big engagement ring, a large solitaire diamond with baguettes on either side, set in platinum, preferably. That ring would come with a handsome man who had a big smile and warm arms that would enfold her in a strong, comforting hug. That ring would symbolize safety and security and it would mean she had the freedom to choose her dreams from inside the delight of a happy marriage. She had been such a dreamer in those days. No such man had materialized and she no longer had any desire for a ring like that. Oh, sure, she wanted the diamonds, but she could buy those any time. The man? Well they always seemed to go to other women.

About an hour out of Toronto the drink trolley came by and Deirdre ordered a coffee.

"Can I bring you anything, Mrs. Reddicoff?" the flight attendant asked gently of the woman seated next to Deirdre.

Reddicoff? Deirdre knew that name from somewhere.

"No, thank you," the woman said.

"I'm so sorry First Class was full," the flight attendant continued.

"Well, it's my own fault, really," Mrs. Reddicoff said amicably. "I didn't tell my assistant about my meeting in Toronto until the last minute. It came up quite suddenly!"

Reddicoff, Reddicoff, Reddicoff, Deirdre was thinking. Where HAD she heard that name?! She furiously searched her memory for details. She usually prided herself on her ability to recall names and places but Reddicoff was not coming up quickly. She was awfully tired. Ever alert to possibility, however, the lawyer in her excused herself from her seat and made her way to the back of the aircraft where the flight attendants were chatting about children's birthday parties and the latest Disney movie.

"Excuse me," Deirdre said, "But who is that Mrs. Reddicoff I'm sitting beside?" She pulled her mouth into the shape of a smile that she hoped would look pleasant.

"Oh she's amazing," one of the attendants gushed. "She and her husband run the largest drill rig manufacturing company in the country and they've just contributed $5 million to fund new equipment for the Calgary children's hospital."

"Five million?" Deirdre asked.

"Yes," the attendant continued in a hushed voice. "She's an engineer, you know.

"Anyway, she and her husband have been married forever and they've got four children — one of them suffers from some kind of heart condition — do you know what it is, Stacy?"

Stacy didn't know.

"Anyway they were so grateful for all the help hospital staff gave them that they decided to make the hospital their number one charity from now on. Isn't she wonderful?"

The flight attendant was clearly impressed with Mrs. Reddicoff. Deirdre was too. Millions of dollars, a great husband and four children. But she didn't look like a successful person! She would make a great client! Had Deirdre blown it? Could she take back her angry, insulting comments and hurtful opinions? Deirdre slipped into the washroom and thought about her mistaken assumptions about the amazing Mrs. Reddicoff. How could she have missed the chance to get to know her? This woman could make her career!

The airplane had begun its descent into Toronto when Deirdre returned to her seat. She smiled quietly at Mrs. Reddicoff as she asked her to move so she could get past her. Mrs. Reddicoff barely glanced at her as she stood up to let her pass. She was busy reading. After she sat down, Deirdre glanced at the paper in front of the woman.

"Dear Mommy," it read. "I love you. Will you please bring me with you next time you go away? Jack has been to Toronto twice now and it's my turn too. Daddy isn't very good at making your special pancakes but he lets us stay up late. Please hurry home. Xxoo Melody."

Deirdre suddenly felt old and tired. There was no child in her life wishing she would make special pancakes for them and there was no man waiting for her to hurry home. She had no rings to symbolize commitment of any sort, temporary or otherwise, and she had just blown the chance to land the best client of her whole career.

She looked out the aircraft window at the light of a morning caught in the dawn of a new day. Mrs. Reddicoff was sitting back in the seat beside her, her eyes closed and a light smile playing on her lips. She looked rested and resilient.

Deirdre shrank in horror at the idea she had missed the cues that might have led her to a good relationship with Mrs. Reddicoff. She was mortally embarrassed to think that she had burned a bridge that could never be rebuilt. Was she doing that in her personal life as well? Was she burning bridges that could lead her to fulfillment and joy, Thursday morning pancakes and a satisfying career?

Deirdre didn't know. There was so much she didn't know. Was there something here she needed to learn? She thought of her lonely condominium and her empty fridge. She thought of all the Christmas Eves she had spent in the office and all the New Year's Eves that were over by 11.

She had no cottage in Canmore to give her delight and no house in Arizona to bring her warmth. Was there maybe a middle way after all? Could she succeed at work while building a family? It didn't seem easy. She didn't know how. Deirdre returned to her briefs but her heart felt heavy.

By the time the wheels of the airplane touched down on a hazy Toronto morning, Deirdre had read everything she needed to review and she was thoughtful. She was ready for her meeting, but was she ready for her life? Was she ready for new risks and new ways of being in the world? She didn't think she was.

But could she *learn* to be ready? It was a scary thought. Mrs. Reddicoff had found a way to balance a successful career with a successful family. Mrs. Reddicoff contributed in massive ways to a community that needed her heart, needed her warmth. Deirdre wasn't sure she had much warmth to share anymore. Was this something she could grow into? Was it something she could enjoy?

Deirdre turned on her Smartphone and looked out the window at a city just starting to awaken. Jared had left a voice mail message on her office phone and she had picked it up just before leaving Calgary. It would be early back in Calgary but the automated attendant at her office switchboard would put her through. She would leave a voice mail, just so he would know she wasn't ignoring him. Just so…what? What then? Deirdre took a deep breath and punched in the numbers. It was taking all her strength to make this call. It was the hardest and most humbling thing she had ever done.

She held her breath while she waited for the connection to go through. She hoped it wasn't too late. She hoped this wasn't a mistake. Suspended between hope and fear, she counted the seconds until she heard his voice

"Jared Kolaptcha" a familiar voice said.

"Hi Jared," she began.

Mrs. Reddicoff smiled.

"Hey Dee," he said.

Implications of Awakening

Conclusions

I lay back against the sturdy trunk of the apple tree and braced my feet against the thick branch in front of me. It was a brilliant late summer afternoon and a light breeze was playing with the leaves that shielded me from view. If I half-closed my eyes I could imagine that those leaves were fairies or sprites, and although I wasn't sure what the difference was, I felt they were surrounding me like a protective umbrella of friends.

This was my refuge, a secret backyard clubhouse I ran to daily to climb on, dream and write. For the four years my family lived in that modest house in London, Ontario, the tree and I were inseparable. I lived almost as much out there in its arms as I did inside at the time, and the experience planted within me a core understanding of the heartbeat of Nature.

In many ways, I had been awakened into a love of Nature at birth. I was born in the town of Dryden, Ontario, a bustling Ontario mill town sprouting off the Trans Canada Highway near the Manitoba border. I have beautiful memories of going fishing or camping as a youngster in the pristine wilderness of Canada's northland – a place where trees and rocks and lakes led to more trees and rocks and lakes. The air was clear and the water transparent, and you could even hear the whispery sound the trees made as they washed the sky with their feathery bristles.

I have always known Nature as both a protective and majestic true-life entity in my life and my sense of how accurate this idea is has only become stronger as I've grown older. Frankly, though, I've also sometimes suspected that such convictions were little more than fanciful notions concocted by a writer with an Anne of Green Gables imagination. The surprising thing is that I've met and read about an awful lot of people in recent years who have encouraged me to believe that this absurd little concept is more fact than fiction. It's no surprise that the animal communicators, tree huggers and shamans I know feel there is a spirit at work in Nature with which we can fundamentally connect.

But the scientists? Give your head a shake. And then shake it again, please. The concept that there is consciousness in all things is just not going to fly down in the frozen food aisle of MY grocery store. Yet.

Work in the field of quantum physics is increasingly delving into the meaning of atomic specks that can be waves and particles, energy and matter, all at the same time. Where this will lead is anyone's guess. At the moment, there is speculation that as we human beings increasingly awaken into the need to safeguard our natural environment, there will be surprising discoveries about the molecular nature of all matter that could point to the existence of a Prime Creator breathing through our entire world.

As I said, I have an Anne of Green Gables imagination.

But it gives me comfort to know that Albert Einstein himself believed that "imagination is more important than knowledge." Even when our imaginations take us places that are perceptively judged "wrong," they give us interesting things about which to think.

I've long noticed that discussions about the existence of God or the possibility that trees have sensibility very often deteriorate into metaphorical mud-slinging contests. I was warned as a young woman that conversation about religion was to be avoided in social situations and I've generally stayed dutifully away. Nothing polarizes a room faster than a disagreement between an atheist and a staunch Catholic, and to me there is something both pointless and unpleasant about debating the issue.

What such a conflict really reflects, though, is how easily we judge people whose concept of the universe does not match our own. And that, to me, gets at the heart of what awakening is really about: letting go of judgement. This doesn't occur on a spiritual level alone. Judgement trickles down into every level of life, through our beliefs about God, of course, but also into our attitude towards the guy at work who just might be gay to the successful neighbour whose skirts seem too short. .

We judge people for the clothes they wear or the habits they have, and as we put ourselves safely at the centre of all that is right and good in the world, we are effectively proclaiming that we are the final arbiters of behaviour, fashion, taste and morality. And while judgement is very useful as a tool for deciding how we are going to *be* in the world, it fails miserably as a tool for generating compassion. While we are busily condemning others for their choices, we are also busy cutting ourselves off from any benefits those choices might generate in our own corner of the world.

Our moments of awakening teach us that there is another approach to the world that is different from the one we've been clinging to with so much vigor. These moments teach us to be more open to possibility and as we release our judgements of ourselves and others, we are also opening ourselves up to receiving the stray gifts that are waiting to float our way. Gifts like appreciation, comfort, wisdom and affection. Connection with others and the strength of community. There is much goodness waiting for us out in that great big world, if we can just open the doors and welcome it in.

Which leads me to something else I've learned about awakenings: they teach us humility. In a competitive world such as ours has become, we win points for being the strongest, smartest, toughest and most capable. Our perseverance is rewarded by better jobs and bigger houses. In the race to afford a smarter refrigerator or a fancier holiday, who cares if the kids are raising themselves in front of the TV or game console? If we take our eyes off the prize, we are going to lose.

Aren't we?

Having been a single mother twice in my life now, I completely understand the stress that goes along with "making ends meet." I know all about self-denial and bill collectors. But I also know that we are all just one cancer diagnosis away from awakening into an appreciation of what is really valuable in this life: a child's smile, a beautiful sunset, a pretty song, a warm hug. The most successful captain of industry and the meekest Dalit in India are equal when they meet on the path leading to the end of their lives. And I've heard that many people come to their End humbly wishing they'd used their life to make a difference, somehow, in the world.

We don't get a "Do-Over."

But as Death is one side of the humility equation, there is, of course, its partner, Birth. Many mothers understand the sweeping awe that overtakes them following the arrival of a child. I know that, for me, awakening into motherhood was the most powerful experience of my life. Each baby that came along renewed my sense of the miracle of creation and the greatness of the gift I had been given. I had a sense that I'd been specially entrusted with the protection and promotion of a life, and that was an extremely humbling experience for me.

But small awakenings can create humility as well, though: my story of how I was unable to direct a stranger to one of the streets in my neighbourhood showed me that there was space for me to pay more attention to my surroundings in my world. I had always prided myself on how observant I was. And now, thanks to that one little awakening, I am even more observant than ever.

Almost all the characters in my short stories have had to grapple with the paradigm shift that an awakening represents and it was interesting, as their author, to watch their experiences. As an observer, it struck me that an awakening is like wandering from a darkness you didn't know was darkness and on into the light. The light might be radiant or it might be dull. But it does its best to shine on the world you thought you knew and help you see things you had previously missed.

Every time I learn something new, the new knowledge affects and transmutes everything else I know. New facets emerge and old certainties fade. It seems to me that this all helps turn Reality into something of a moving target. This came strongly to light recently when my oldest daughter and I were discussing an incident that had happened when she was three. Four or five of my crystal wine glasses had been broken and I was heartbroken. My daughter, now 25, said she has often felt terrible about having broken those glasses, even though it had been an accident.

I looked at her in shock. "But Heather," I said. "*I* was the one who broke the glasses!"

In that instant, her entire understanding of who she was changed from having been "a little girl who broke Mommy's treasured wine glasses" to "a little girl who DIDN'T break those glasses" and she was released from 22 years of guilt. Not only did her memory of the event shift, but her sense of identity had to change in order to absorb this new information about herself. It was remarkable.

And so we dance. We dance with our understanding of what Reality is, we dance with our memories. We dance with humility and judgement and releasing old paradigms that don't serve us anymore. And we dance with what presents. But somehow in all that dancing, as we sit watching the leaves on the trees or our children's smiles, we are also engaged in the ever-evolving mystery of life and death, the beginnings that are also endings and the endings that bear the promise of a new beginning.

When I was a child listening to the whispers of the trees in my ears, I never could have imagined a thought quite so big. But it seems to me that I would have liked it anyway. I would have leaned back against the comforting trunk of that timeless old apple tree, half-shut my eyes, and watched the spritely leaves whirl above my head. I would have thought about beginnings and endings and how connected they all were. "Ah," I would have thought. "I guess that means there just might be such a thing as 'Forever.'"

Ah yes, little girl. I guess there just might be.

– *Susan Crossman*

About the Author

Susan Crossman is a freelance writer with several decades of experience in the fields of journalism, government communications, PR and marketing and her focus these days lies in the creation of business documents that build reputations and inspire commitment.

Although the work is intriguing and satisfying, she's found that inside the heart of her professional approach to words beats the jungle drum of a creative writer.

Susan currently juggles her freelance writing work with the care of two young children and in the rare moments when she is sure no-one is looking, she sneaks off to wrestle with the untidy task of writing for fun. The result has been the publication in 2011 of several essays in the Globe and Mail.

The fall of 2011 marked the release of **Shades of Teale**, her novel about a woman's journey through marriage to divorce. And the fall of 2012 marked the release of her non-fiction book **Passages to Epiphany**.

Susan is a Master Practitioner of Neurolinguistic Programming (NLP), an expert in social media marketing and search engine optimization, and an awfully strong supporter of the value of chocolate as a medicinal agent. She is fluent in French and Spanish, completely comfortable with possibility and imperfection and absolutely useless with a vacuum. You can find out more information about Susan's business writing and creative writing by visiting: www.crossmancommunications.com

Passages to Epiphany

Manor House Publishing
www.manor-house.biz
905-648-2193

www.ingramcontent.com/pod-product-compliance
Lightning Source LLC
Chambersburg PA
CBHW021111080526
44587CB00010B/479